THE CENTRAL HIGHLANDS

Capel Mounth signpost, Glen Muick

THE CENTRAL HIGHLANDS

Six Long Distance Walks

by

P.D. Koch-Osborne

CICERONE PRESS
MILNTHORPE, CUMBRIA

© P.D. Koch-Osborne 1998
ISBN 1 85284 267 9
A catalogue record for this book is available from the British Library

*This book is dedicated to my wife, Eileen
who has not only accompanied me on all the research but has
typed the manuscript and uncomplainingly assisted with the
whole enterprise. Without such support and help the task
would have been a lone campaign indeed.*

Advice to Readers

Readers are advised that whilst every effort is taken by the author to ensure the accuracy of this guidebook, changes can occur which may affect the contents. It is advisable to check locally on transport, accommodation, shops etc but even rights-of-way can be altered.

The publisher would welcome notes of any such changes

Other Cicerone books by the same author:

The Scottish Glens Book 1 - Cairngorm Glens
Book 2 - the Atholl Glens
Book 3 - The Glens of Rannoch
Book 4 - The Glens of Trossach
Book 5 - The Glens of Argyll
Book 6 - The Great Glen
Book 7 - The Angus Glens

Front cover: Ben Alder from Culra Glen

CONTENTS

The gate before Victoria Bridge (Walk 1)

THE CENTRAL HIGHLANDS OF SCOTLAND
Area covered by guide

INTRODUCTION

THE OBJECTS OF THIS BOOK

Quite obviously the prime object is to guide, to provide a means, an idea, a starting point for others to set out to enjoy a few days in our wild places. This book is therefore a means for me to pass on the benefit of my local knowledge to inspire others to enjoy, as I have done, the experience of travelling considerable distances on self-planned expeditions on foot.

The underlying object of this book may not be so obvious. Scotland is crossed by many rights of way, some little used. These are not shown on O.S. maps but their regular use is needed to maintain these established routes. Their existence and exact routing is not always accurately enough defined to map properly. Also, if the rights of way were mapped, this may lead to restrictions on other paths and tracks. The present delicate balance between walker, landowner and rights of way maintains reasonably free access, outwith the stalking seasons. Too accurate definition of these ways, bad conduct of visitors, and a lack of understanding of the working landscape can all upset this delicate balance. Only considerable use will keep these rights of way open.

Virtually all the paths and tracks given on the following pages are on rights of way. However, a healthy respect for the landowner must be maintained - even on a right of way you are on his or her land! I make no apology for repeating this message in the following pages.

A further object of this book is to spread the pressure created by too many visitors concentrated in one area - the environmentally damaging 'honeypot' effect. Tens of thousands tramp the West Highland Way each year. It is too busy. It is also within earshot of a trunk road for much of its length; this is not wilderness. Its usage creates erosion problems and too much pressure on accommodation along one 'corridor'. It may be a good introduction to backpacking but what next? I hope the routes depicted in the following pages provide some of the answers - a stepping stone to a greater appreciation of the wild places.

CONSERVATION

Scotland is not an outdoor gymnasium, with Munros, Corbetts, Donalds, Great Walks, Big Walks, Huge Walks, all waiting to be 'done' or 'bagged' and ticked off in a book. Wild Scotland is a working landscape of deer forest, grouse moor, hill sheep farms, beef and dairy farms, and commercial forest. There is money to be made from the necessary shooting of deer, and the unnecessary shooting of grouse. Moves are afoot to regenerate parts of the Caledonian Forest, even to introduce wolves. Red Kite and Osprey are back. Conservation is starting to work. Scotland is a managed wilderness, not a playground.

Another delicate balance exists between landowners and conservation groups, both now very often having similar objectives. Visitors who appreciate the working landscape are welcome; the 'gymnast' is regarded with understandable suspicion. This book is not for the 'gymnast'.

CONDUCT

I should like to think this section is not necessary. Still, litter is dropped, bothies are vandalised, stiles, gates and dykes damaged. Who does these things and what, if anything, are these people thinking about?

As lovers of the wild places we must behave, ask permission for access where appropriate, and generally be polite. No-one ever won an argument with a stalker! If access is unreasonably refused - by signpost or by word of mouth - comply with the request. If you feel aggrieved contact the Scottish Rights of Way Society and the landowner, but do it with dignity! Any other approach results in a hardening of attitudes in both camps and 'no access' is the result.

Stalking seasons

Red deer	-	1 July to 20 October (stags)
		21 October to 15 February (hinds)
Grouse	-	12 August (glorious 12th!) to 10 December

(Both the above are at their most intensive from mid August to mid October with hind shooting parties common at Christmas and New Year).

Lambing	-	Mid April to end of May.

Scottish sheep are not used to coping with the sight of strange dogs
- even on a lead.

During these dates it is essential to stick to rights of way and
polite to check at the local lodges to ensure you are not interfering
with the estate's activities. Refer to the Highland seasons chart
(p19).

NAVIGATION
Navigation in the glens is not to be underestimated. A sound
knowledge of the use of map and compass is needed and, just as
importantly, experience of speed of travel is needed to judge
distances over varying terrain. Many navigating mistakes are made,
not through an ignorance of where north is, but losing position due
to errors in distance travelled. Scottish glens are long, and many as
high as English hilltops. Navigation and distance estimation should
be well practised before either are needed for real. Gain experience
in judging the size of rivers from the region's rainfall and look at the
map to assess the area they drain. Relate this to current weather
conditions.

RIVERS
The crossing of Scottish rivers requires consideration not applicable
in England and Wales. In Scotland there are much larger areas of
wild country, higher rainfall (especially in the west) and snow-melt.
Hot sun in May can cause flood conditions from fast melting and
largely unseen snow. This can cause rivers to rise during the course
of the day to double their size, and to fall again during the night as
the thaw slows, or ceases as snow re-freezes.

There is no substitute for experience in judging the size of rivers
from a) the area they drain on the map (count the grid squares) b)
the rainfall and c) the prevailing conditions, rain, snow-melt or
drought. Bridges shown on O.S. maps are not always there so it is
folly to rely on a bridge without an alternative route in mind. The
routes in this book describe river crossings where they occur but
conditions vary! Bridges shown in the following pages may
disappear.

River crossing procedure is as follows. Remove boots and socks.
Put boots on bare feet. Cross - pick a wide, shallow area if possible.
Replace dry socks, drain boots and replace. Snow-melt is so cold it

hurts, so in these conditions socks and gaiters help against the cold - provided you have spare socks to change into. Hold onto each other - in threes is best - and above all don't take risks. Roped river crossings are beyond the scope of this book and require specialist equipment and knowledge.

MOUNTAINS

One of my favourite ways of enjoying the wild places is to choose a 'through' route of, say, 3 days' duration, stay 2 nights at one location on the way and include a mountain walk without a full pack. Surely the most satisfying mountain day is one enjoyed when both starting and finishing at a bothy or wild camp. Mountain walks are suggested as an adjunct to the 'through' walks but please note:

1) Mountain safety, navigation and equipment and a knowledge of its application should be faultless.

2) In these circumstances it may not be possible to tell anyone where you are or your estimated time of arrival so - care!

3) A minimum safe number in summer is three. Such a trip in winter is a serious mountaineering expedition.

4) Once you take to the summits you are off rights of way - so ask permission if you can.

5) A wild camp - especially of more than one night - needs permission.

SAFETY

The walks depicted comprise anything from a pleasant summer amble to a serious winter expedition and safety considerations should reflect the season and the nature of the walk. Always leave word of your route, think twice before travelling alone (and never in winter), always take a survival bag, spare food, spare clothing, whistle, map, torch (with spare batteries and bulb) and compass.

This book should be studied (of course!) before setting out, together with maps, possible 'escape' routes and the general level of rivers, especially if swollen by snow-melt.

SCOTTISH WEATHER

No! it doesn't rain all the time - but don't tell anyone or Scotland will fill up with tourists! Most of the rain falls in the west and 'showers' can mean continuous rain in Lochaber and a fine day in the Cairngorms! Snow can fall in any month of the year. Blizzards are possible from October to May and in winter can last up to 4 days.

I have sunbathed (on the Grey Corries ridge) in shorts and T-shirt at 1100m on one day and suffered howling wind and sleet at low level the next - in May! Be prepared - make sure you have sound waterproofs and go in May or June.

If your trip has to be in July or August go east and take plenty of midge repellent. Use the forecasts, however inaccurate, and keep an eye out for freshening wind and clouds building up on the horizon. Don't be too quick to dismiss a forecast as wrong - often just the timing of the passage of weather fronts is inaccurate.

The effect of the sun should not be underestimated. Even in these northern latitudes an effective sun screen and covering for the head and back of the neck should always be used in full sun.

FIRST AID
This is not a book about first aid but a kit should always be carried - and some knowledge is useful - if only to ease living with blisters or the odd sprain. I once used up an entire first aid kit on a friend who fell off a scramble in the Lake District, but the temporary repairs enabled him to walk to a road with help. Whether coping with a disaster or easing a blister it is best to be prepared.

EXPOSURE
Linked with exhaustion, exposure can be a killer - even in the glens. Wind and driving rain can be as dangerous as full winter conditions. The secret is not to be caught unawares by the weather. Sufficient clothing should be taken to stay warm (whilst inactive) in the worst weather you are likely to encounter. Multiple thin layers are better than thick ones - some of the huge walking jackets on sale today are just too big to carry.

The effects of exposure manifest themselves as feeling cold, tired, out of character behaviour, failure to respond or communicate properly, defective vision, slurring of speech (as if drunk), violent shivering, temper, sudden outbursts of new-found energy, stumbling, falling, cramps, eventually unconsciousness, coma -

11

death.

The sufferer must be sheltered from the wind and physically warmed, possibly by sharing a sleeping bag, and medical help must be sought.

I have only once had to treat exposure - a young cyclist on the Outer Hebrides in July, soaking wet, stumbling and falling and with slurred speech on arrival at a hostel. Fortunately, the several people present all knew what to do. This also proves you don't need to be on a mountain top in winter to suffer exposure. Always be alert to the possibility of it.

ACCOMMODATION

The individual route summaries show distances between accommodation (B&B or hostel). These should be sought out by contacting Tourist Information. Advance booking will be needed in July and August and most tourist facilities close, annoyingly, just before the English October half-term school holiday until, sometimes, after Easter.

Pre-booking may commit you to a long day out in adverse conditions and I prefer to avoid this, yet another reason to favour May/June as there is less need to book during these months.

TRAVEL TO/FROM THE START/FINISH

The walks are deliberately planned around continuous rights of way starting and finishing at points where trains, or at least a decent bus service, are available. One can also start and end at a B&B or similar. A car is a severely limiting factor when planning a long distance walking trip and it is best left at home.

USE OF BOTHIES

Many of the longer stretches of wild country are provided with bothies, many maintained by the Mountain Bothies Association (MBA). These buildings require treating with the utmost respect and are owned by the estates, often deliberately left open as emergency shelter. Never leave litter or use the last of the firewood without replacing it. Always leave it cleaner than you find it, and shut the door so no animals can seek shelter and starve to death if the door blows shut! Users of bothies should join the MBA and support their maintenance through the very reasonable annual fee and by practical help.

WILD CAMPING
Permission must always be sought if you intend to camp wild in Scotland. The excellent book *Heading for the Scottish Hills*, compiled by the Mountaineering Council of Scotland and the Scottish Landowners' Federation, explains who owns what and gives telephone numbers. The estates do appreciate being asked and 'keepers don't bite your head off! Contact improves walker/ landowner relations whilst no contact combined with an "I've a right to go anywhere" attitude (which you haven't!) does untold damage!

STAYING DRY
A full set of good waterproofs is essential - overtrousers and a breathable cagoule or jacket with a hood. It is essential that the trunk of the body is kept warm and dry. Anything else is miserable at best and potentially dangerous at worst.

A change of inner layers should be carried. Your pack should have a liner or a cover - a bin liner will do but use a strong one if it is to last a few days. There's nothing to beat leather boots and gaiters for keeping feet dry - in midsummer gaiters can be dispensed with but are still useful in deep heather. If you use fabric boots for lightness, even 'waterproof' ones, prepare for wet feet. Try to plan major river crossings near the end of a day if possible.

EQUIPMENT
What to take and what not to take becomes the result of experience of many sorties. The following is a list of what you will need to take plus a few tips and hints intended to avoid some of the common pitfalls.

Item	Tips
Rucksack	Must have a pelvic harness
Rucksack liner or cover	A bin bag will do
Stove/fuel	Consider weight, safety, speed
Cooking pan(s) & handle	Use also as plates

Item	Tips
Sleeping bag (+ liner)	In Scotland 3-season minimum or 1-season plus fleece liner
Sleeping mat	Hip length in summer, use clothes as pillow/extra padding
Tent (unless known bothies/hostels etc. to be used)	Don't skimp on tent size - make savings elsewhere
Maps	1:50,000 Ordnance Survey
Whistle	Tie permanently to rucksack
Torch	Preferably a head-torch. Include spare batteries and bulb
Compass	Plus knowledge in its correct use
Day food packs	Plus one day spare
Boots	Plus gaiters for winter/wet
Socks	Plus spare socks
Underwear (thermal)	Plus spares
Shirt and sweatshirt	Better than 2 shirts - can be worn together in emergency/cold
Fleece jacket	(or two in winter)
Waterproof shell jacket	I prefer a lightweight shell to a heavy jacket, plus 2 fleeces - more flexible
Breeches or 'longs' - heavy	Or lightweight plus long thermal underwear
Overtrousers	Must go on over boots
Gloves, hat, scarf	For quick temperature adjustment 'on the hoof'
Survival bag	Plus knowledge of correct use
First Aid kit	Plus knowledge of correct use
Spare laces	Handy for all sorts of repairs
Spares for stove, spanner etc.	Always test stove before setting out
Matches	Plus spares sealed in film container
Soap, toothbrush	Both cut in half or travel toothbrush
Toothpaste	Keep a nearly used tube or collect samples
Towel	Small - the pertex ones are OK if used in warm weather, otherwise miserably cold

Item	Tips
Water sterilizing tablets	Keep in a tin or film container
Measuring liquids	Punch sides of a pan to use as a measuring jug. Know the volume of your plastic mug and other containers
Mini transistor radio	Essential for weather forecast updates. Stick a label on the radio giving weather forecast times/ waveband details etc. - and use it!

The following are items you can probably do without (especially in summer).

Item	Tips
Flask	Use a quick boil stove
Plates and dishes	Use your pan set (also takes less washing up if scraped out by a hungry walker!)
Knives and forks	One knife should do. Most of your food can be spooned
Folding washing up bowl	Use your pan
Heavy un-packable jacket	Two fleeces plus a waterproof shell is more flexible and easier to pack
Bivvy bag (other than emergency)	Neither use nor ornament in Scottish weather!
Most of packaging for the food you take	See section on food planning
Towel	Use pertex in hot weather or 'drip dry'. A thermal vest can be used as a towel, washed, wrung out and dried (in good weather) by the next day
Cooking utensils	One knife for the whole group, one fork plus a spoon each
Measuring jug	Mark existing containers

If you end up with an enormous pile of gear weighing half a ton you've got something wrong!

These suggestions do not cater for winter conditions on the mountains. A winter backpack involves extra gear, ice axes, crampons, rope etc., specialist knowledge and experience and the fitness to carry everything - quickly as daylight is very limited. I would recommend venturing on a serious winter expedition only with a very experienced party who fully appreciate what they are undertaking.

DRINKING WATER

It is important to maintain a high fluid intake to avoid dehydration. Water should always be boiled, or sterilized if used cold. Many profess to have never had any trouble drinking stream water but the sight of a dead deer in a stream (common because they seek the shelter of trees and a ravine when weak) makes me think twice. I use simple sterilizing tablets - they're easy to carry and you (almost) get used to the taste. More sophisticated systems are available but they all have to be carried and some are quite expensive.

FOOD PLANNING

The haphazard bundling of food into a rucksack can result in unnecessary weight being carried and an unbalanced diet - or worse still a food shortage towards the end of the trip. After purchasing food, for, say a 5 day expedition, my wife and I pack this into day packs. Each parcel contains 24 hours' food, including snacks, to form a day's food, balancing freeze dried with fresh food.

Start by removing most of the packaging - but not the cooking instructions - and re-packing 2 breakfasts, 2 elevenses, 2 lunches, 2 afternoon snacks, 2 main meals and 2 suppers into each parcel, finishing off with a cling film wrapping. Each day's food for two will take up the space of a small shoe box. Always go for food with the shortest (fuel-saving) cooking time.

Open the day's food at the same time each day. This method makes re-packing rucksacks easy and although requiring pre-planning, actually saves time and weight when enjoying those valuable days in the wild country. Again, experience fine-tunes your individual methods and requirements.

COOKING

The choice of stove is one of personal preference. I use petrol. It requires treating with great respect and the fuel needs storing well away from food - in a separate rucksack if possible. The petrol stove is heavy but is quick enough to save carrying flasks for a hot drink mid-day. The high calorific value of the fuel means fuel for a longer trip weighs less.

The speed of the stove tends to cook faster than I can eat but it is controllable. Meths-fuelled companions are usually starting their soup as I finish my meal with a coffee! A fast stove means a quick start in the mornings - more time to enjoy the walking!

LITTER

Never, never, never leave any litter. Even biodegradable matter looks a mess while it degrades. Banana skins and rotting orange peel detract from the feeling of isolation we seek in the wild places. Burnable rubbish can go on a bothy fire but when the food packages are prepared as described above there is little rubbish and it is easily carried out. There is no excuse for leaving anything.

Litter should be re-packed into clean parcels. I find a typical day's litter packs into a tennis-ball sized package which when re-wrapped in the cling film from the day's food parcel is easily carried out and disposed of at home. Also don't be too proud to pick up someone else's litter or take a bit of extra rubbish away from a bothy - as a responsible walker it **is** something to do with you.

TOILET TRAINING

The disposal of human waste is a major problem with increasing numbers spending more than a day in the wild country. Problems occur around popular bothies and wild camping locations. There are certain rules that can be followed to ease the problem of pollution.

Firstly try to organise your routine ('body clock') so you defecate in the middle of the day when miles away from a bothy or camp location - or water supply. (This gets more difficult as the consumption of backpackers' freeze dried food increases - or any food which induces the 'sudden dash syndrome'!)

When you have to go, don't just lift a rock and replace it, leaving paper sticking out from under it as a trade mark - that's revolting.

Tested methods are as follows:

1) If, and only if, miles from anywhere, spread the excrement about to maximise exposure to air and rapid decomposition. The paper can be very carefully burnt but don't set the whole hillside alight.

2) If you have eaten a freeze dried meal, and you are in a bothy and it's dark and the 'sudden dash syndrome' manifests itself, go as far away from the bothy/tent/water supply as time allows and dig a hole. Use a flat stone to dig - a shovel is too heavy to lug around the hills but is sometimes provided in bothies. You will have decided upon a 'designated area' before it gets dark.

3) Woods often have deep sphagnum moss. This is toilet luxury - a handful provides not only a hole but biodegradable damp toilet tissue!

FITNESS

Trying to bite off more than one can chew can be miserable. With a heavy pack start off by doing 13-16km (8-10 miles) in a day. Thirty-two kilometres (20 miles) with a full pack is a comfortable limit for just about anyone - excluding the super fit. Rough ground, weather, river crossings or lying snow can wreak havoc with one's ability to cover distance.

Try to aim at comfortable distances and build up to longer distances if you want to increase your potential for undertaking more committing routes. Setting too high a target leads to fatigue, misery and a return to more sedentary pastimes! It is assumed that before undertaking a backpacking trip of several days' duration one is fit enough to walk all day with a reasonably heavy pack - a lower fitness level is a liability.

NOTES FOR WALKER'S CALENDAR (see chart)

1) Grouse and deer stalking limits access to rights of way only (or other areas only by permission).

2) Lambing limits access to rights of way only, in some areas, and other areas by permission (in sheep farming areas). Dogs even on a lead are not to be taken. A loose dog may be shot!

3) Wild country backpacking is best in May or June, or late

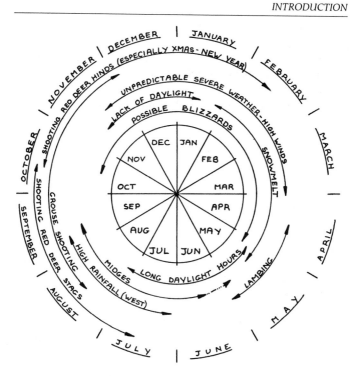

September/early October if rights of way are strictly adhered to. These also happen to be the best months for photography.

4) Winter backpacking hasn't a lot going for it - unless it is a properly organised expedition with time to wait for a 'window' in the weather.

5) Generally rain, snow, wind (and midges) are more severe in the west. The exception is the Cairngorms where storms are legendary.

6) Scotland's reputation for rain and midges is based on a West Coast July/August tourist season - two months to avoid in my opinion!

7) The rewards for timing a backpacking trip right are long, long

19

days in perfect weather with hardly a soul to be seen, away from traffic, fumes, pollution, telephones, noise and hassle! Magic.

MAPS

The maps on the following pages are not intended to be a substitute for the O.S. maps. It is important that the relevant O.S. maps are taken on any walks.

My sketch maps provide additional information relevant to the walks described, and unnecessary repetition of information given on the O.S. maps, other than for location, has been avoided. All the routes given, and all paths and tracks connecting with these routes, have been carefully surveyed by me (well -someone has to do it!) and graded as set out on the map key. Some grading anomalies are bound to occur but you should at least know in advance what is to be encountered under foot.

The O.S. maps are extremely inaccurate when it comes to hill and glen paths and tracks although these features are something of a 'moving target' to keep up with as new tracks appear, old tracks disappear under the heather and new paths are trodden out by walkers. Bridges also disappear - be warned!

The walks have distance indicators showing accumulated distance from the start. These also serve as reference points in the text.

Minor burns and fords and contours are omitted from the maps - these can be ascertained from the O.S. maps. However, I have commented on larger fords and alternatives if crossing is impossible or dangerous.

Paths and tracks on old railway lines are graded as usual but with the addition of 'sleepers'.

CONCLUSION

The purpose of this introduction has been to highlight some key areas which will enable you to enjoy the wild places in safety whilst leaving no trace of your passing, so those who follow are able to enjoy the same pristine wilderness. It would be possible to write a book under each of the above headings - indeed this has already been done! The above notes are not exhaustive, but intended to avoid some of the pitfalls and provide a base that can be built on by both further study (ie. first aid) and experience.

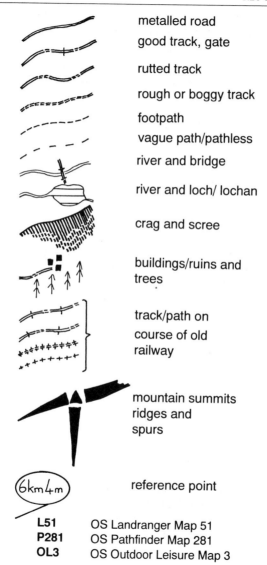

metalled road

good track, gate

rutted track

rough or boggy track

footpath

vague path/pathless

river and bridge

river and loch/ lochan

crag and scree

buildings/ruins and
trees

track/path on
course of old
railway

mountain summits
ridges and
spurs

reference point

L51   OS Landranger Map 51
P281   OS Pathfinder Map 281
OL3   OS Outdoor Leisure Map 3

WALK 1:
Taynuilt to Dalwhinnie

This is a superb cross-country walk of some 117km (72.5 miles). It starts by Loch Etive and Glen Kinglass, passing Loch Tulla and skirting Rannoch Moor via Gorton to Bridge of Gaur before climbing once again to Loch Ericht. The high pass of Bealach Dubh, in the heart of Ben Alder Forest, is literally the high point of the walk before following the shore of Loch Ericht to Dalwhinnie.

The above route is to be preferred to the 'short cut' following Loch Ericht for almost its entire 27km (17 mile) length. However, maps 22 and 23 are shown in case weather conditions rule out the high bealach.

I have suggested a west to east direction as this keeps both the prevailing wind and afternoon sun behind you.

Both ends of the walk (and off the route at Bridge of Orchy and

Walk 1: Taynuilt to Dalwhinnie

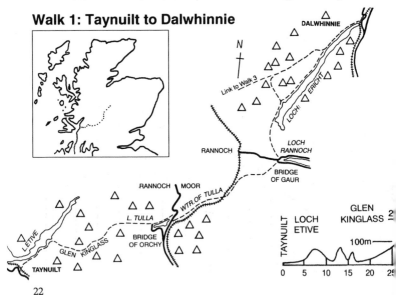

Rannoch) have railway stations and bus services, so public transport access is no problem - even if you have to bail out half way!

There is an almost complete lack of accommodation or civilization throughout this walk - which is surely the reason for doing it. Walkers have, therefore, to be totally self-reliant, carrying both food and shelter, though bothies are indicated.

Public roads are encountered only at Victoria Bridge and the Water of Tulla crossing on the A82 (both near Bridge of Orchy); and Bridge of Gaur (for Rannoch).

It should be noted that between Bealach Cumhann and Bealach Dubh on map 17 a short pathless connection links into a path leading to Strath Ossian, therefore linking up to Walk 2 for a return to Fort William. In this case a car could be left at Tyndrum using the Lower station outward to Taynuilt and the Upper returning from Fort William.

Access to several mountain groups, most notably the southern reaches of the Ben Starav group, Ben Alder and Aonach Beag, are possible from the through route. This provides what is in my view the perfect mountain day: starting and ending in the wild.

Gradient profile:
Taynuilt to Dalwhinnie

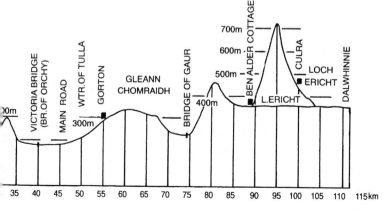

Diagrammatical index to maps

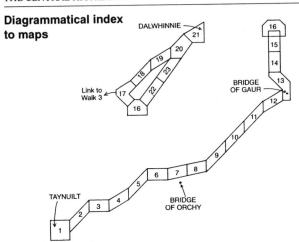

Walk 1: Taynuilt to Dalwhinnie - at a glance guide

Length:	117km (72.5 miles) - Loch Ericht path (reduces this by 5km or 3 miles). 5 to 7 days
Total climbing:	approximately 1250m (reduced to 900m by the Loch Ericht path)
Accommodation:	Bothies and wild camping
Roads at:	Taynuilt 0km Bridge of Awe (near) 6km (4 miles) Victoria Bridge 40km (25 miles) Loch Tulla 46km (29 miles) Bridge of Gaur 75km (46.5 miles) Dalwhinnie 117km (72.5 miles)
Bus services at:	Taynuilt 0km Bridge of Orchy (6km or 4 miles off the route) Bridge of Gaur (postbus) 75km (46.5 miles) Dalwhinnie 117km (72.5 miles)
Rail services at:	Taynuilt 0km Bridge of Orchy (6km or 4 miles off the route) Rannoch (9km or 6 miles from Bridge of Gaur at 75km or 46.5 miles) Dalwhinnie 117km (72.5 miles)

Access *to mountain groups en route:*
                Ben Cruachan
                Ben Starav group
                Stob Gobhar and the Black Mount
                Ben Alder and Aonach Beag groups

O.S. maps (in their order of appearance):
                Landranger 50, 51, 42
                Pathfinder, 332, 319, 320, 321, 307, 292, 279, 266, 267

MAP 1. TAYNUILT

Starting from Taynuilt railway station the walk covers 4km (2.5 miles) of road to the River Awe crossing. This is unavoidable unless transport is available to the start of the track at 6km (4 miles).

On leaving the main road and crossing under the railway, at

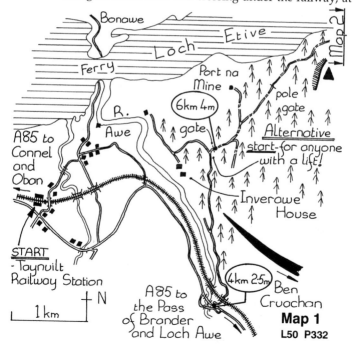

4km, (2.5 miles) the minor road follows the route of the old military road, shown on Roy's Military Survey of 1755, and a part of the Inveraray to Bonawe and Tyndrum military road. At 6km (4 miles) turn right through a gate onto a forest road which will soon pick up the right of way alongside Loch Etive.

Over the slight rise which is the low western spur of Ben Cruachan, ignore firstly the new forest road joining from the right and secondly the left branch to Port na Mine.

A gradual descent brings the track down to the lochside and the right of way is joined just after a pole gate. In theory the right of way runs west along the lochside to Dun Mor, but much of this is overgrown.

MAP 2. GLENNOE
Continuing along the lochside the track threads its way around the outflow of the River Noe at Glennoe at 11km

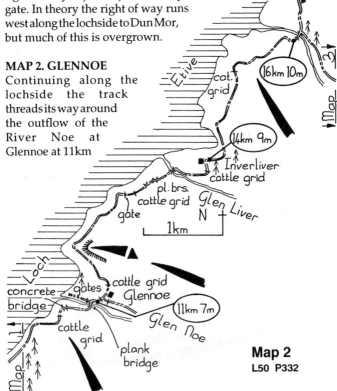

Map 2
L50 P332

(7 miles), climbing around the headland below A Chruach. This section reveals fine views up and down Loch Etive and after 11km or so who needs an excuse for a rest?

It is interesting to note that we are now on the new track to Glen Kinglass. Originally the track used to end at Glennoe and the connection to the start of Glen Kinglass was by path only. Vehicular access to Ardmaddy was by Glen Kinglass, and Inverliver was accessible on foot or by boat only.

Another tortuous section by-passes Inverliver at 14km (9 miles). Note the strange perched boulder in the wood on the right. Beyond Inverliver the last good views up and down Loch Etive are noted before the headland is crossed into the start of Glen Kinglass.

The long plank bridge is crossed at 16km (10 miles) and a right turn taken for the Glen Kinglass track. Here the rights of way divide and straight ahead the track, which soon after Ardmaddy degenerates into a rough path, heads for the public road in Glen Etive, some 13km (8.5 miles) from the bridge. We turn right.

MAP 3. NARRACHAN

Once into Glen Kinglass the scene changes. After a rough start through birchwoods the track soon improves. About 300m from the junction of the tracks the O.S. Pathfinder map depicts: Furnace (disused). This is the ruin of iron ore smelting operations which

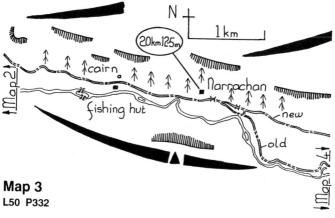

Map 3
L50 P332

Narrachan

were in operation in the early eighteenth century using ore brought by sea from Ulverston in what was then Lancashire but is now Cumbria. Local timber from the neighbouring glens was used in the furnace.

After 2km (1.2 miles) Lady Wyfold's cairn is passed, opposite a small fishing hut. At 20km (12.5 miles) Narrachan is reached. The bothy was once part of a small thatched or turf-roofed community, evident from the surrounding ruins and the old roof timbers of Narrachan. The rounded corners of the building reveal its 'black house' origins, although one end has a later gable and chimney.

Soon after Narrachan the track divides, the old riverside track being more interesting to walk as well as being the right of way. The new track was built because of river bank erosion.

MAP 4. GLENKINGLASS LODGE

At 22.5km (14 miles) the ruin at Acharn is reached. Here the new track rejoins the old and on the right a suspension bridge marks the start of the right of way over to neighbouring Glen Strae, in turn part of the route from Dalmally to Glencoe via Glen Strae, Glen Kinglass and Glen Etive. This path also provides access to Beinn Eunaich

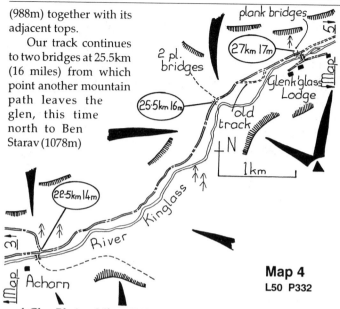

(988m) together with its adjacent tops.

Our track continues to two bridges at 25.5km (16 miles) from which point another mountain path leaves the glen, this time north to Ben Starav (1078m)

plank bridges

27km 17m

Glenk'glass Lodge

2 pl. bridges

25.5km 16m

old track

N

1km

22.5km 14m

Kinglass

River

Map 3

Achorn

Map 4
L50 P332

and Glas Bheinn Mhor (993m). Beinn nan Aighenan (957m) lies immediately to the right of this path.

The next bridge is opposite Glenkinglass Lodge at 27km (17 miles). The Lodge is normally occupied and the track is not maintained beyond here as the climb to the watershed begins in earnest.

Suspension bridge

29

MAP 5. LOCH DOCHARD

The rough track crosses two suspension bridges, the second being at 30km (19 miles). The path can be wet and is easy to

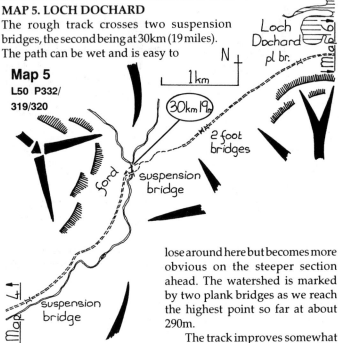

Map 5

L50 P332/
319/320

lose around here but becomes more obvious on the steeper section ahead. The watershed is marked by two plank bridges as we reach the highest point so far at about 290m.

The track improves somewhat on its descent to Loch Dochard as superb views to the mountains of the Black Mount open up to the north.

MAP 6. CLASHGOUR

At the far end of Loch Dochard are two buildings: one a locked fishing hut, the other an open stable which would provide temporary shelter from wind and rain if required.

The descent continues to the fords below Clashgour which can be avoided by taking the suspension bridge on the left to cross the Abhainn Shira, and the plank bridge over the Allt Ghabhar at 36km (22 miles).

The right of way continues along the river bank as a path, not the track via Glasghour, although I have cycled via Glashgour without objection.

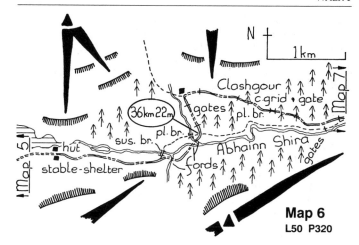

Map 6
L50 P320

The track is rejoined as it emerges on our left through a gate. A Scottish Rights of Way Society signpost confirms our use of the riverside path.

MAP 7. VICTORIA BRIDGE
The tiny Clashgour hut is passed on the left as the track winds its way to Victoria Bridge at 40km (25 miles). The view in retrospect from the gate is worth a photograph - you won't be the first to capture

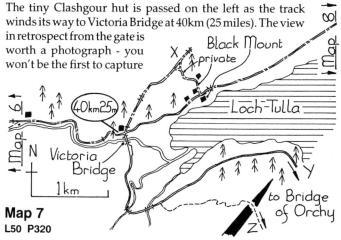

Map 7
L50 P320

this superb view on film!

Victoria Bridge has been a major river crossing and road junction for centuries. Here the north-south route is crossed. Once a drove road, this was replaced by the military road in about 1750. The military road is shown on the O.S. map above the West Highland Way north of Loch Tulla, and taking the direct line to Bridge of Orchy south of Loch Tulla.

The next road lasted from the early nineteenth century until the 1930s and comprises what is now the West Highland Way north of Loch Tulla, and the A8005 from Victoria Bridge to Bridge of Orchy. Indeed this rather odd bit of A-class road is a remnant of the 1930 main road.

The present-day A82 crosses the old road at Bridge of Orchy and continues around the east end of Loch Tulla. The old main road has been put to good use as the West Highland Way, a good introduction to the long cross-country walk such as Taynuilt to Dalwhinnie - but too busy!

Our route lies straight ahead past Black Mount along the north shore of Loch Tulla. This bit is not a right of way but I received no worse than a friendly wave when I cycled along it.

The diversion via Bridge of Orchy adds 4km (2.5 miles) (what price a shower and a pint followed by a warm bed!)

MAP 8. ACHALLADER

We emerge at Tulla Cottage. Here we are obliged to head south for 1km (half a mile) to the start of the track to Gorton at 46km (29 miles). Those who succumbed to the comforts of the Bridge of Orchy Hotel will head north on the main road, picking up the old drove road about 1km north of the village. This runs between road and railway - under the pylons.

The track continues to Augh-Chalada (now Achallader), once a large village. Note its ancient tower and unique turf-topped walls.

Keeping to the left of Achallader the track continues up Water of Tulla. By-pass the fords on the left and cross the river at the bridge opposite the sad but substantial ruined house of Barravourich.

Here the ford track rejoins from the left and with Barravourich ahead, we turn right through a gate to continue on the track to Gorton.

Above Victoria Bridge (Walk 1)
Culra and Lancet Edge (Walk 1)

The track above Glennoe (Walk 1)
Aonach Beag from Geal Charn (Walk 1)

Map 8
L50 P320

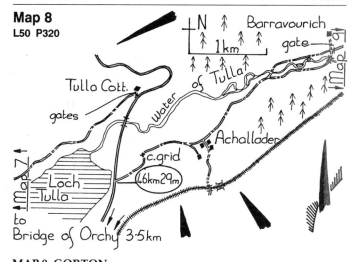

gate

1 km

Tulla Cott.

gates

Water of Tulla

Achallader

Map 7

c.grid

(4·6km 29m)

Loch
Tulla

Map 9

to
Bridge of Orchy 3·5km

MAP 9. GORTON

Gorton Bothy at 55km (34 miles) is a welcome sight after the long walk up Water of Tulla. Here the track ends and some care in navigating is needed over the next few kilometres.

The path east of Gorton soon becomes vague and the obvious route appears to be to cross the railway by the underpass near the site of Rowantree Cottage. Indeed a path can be seen passing under the railway at this point. However, the footbridge shown across Water of Tulla 500m east of Gorton no longer exists and the right of way continues east, north of the river, for 2.5km (1.5 miles).

Gorton bothy

North of this vague path is Madagan Moineach, a drovers' stance where cattle bound for the markets of Crieff or Falkirk were rested overnight. The drovers' route came by Loch Treig (long before its level was raised), east of Loch Laidon,

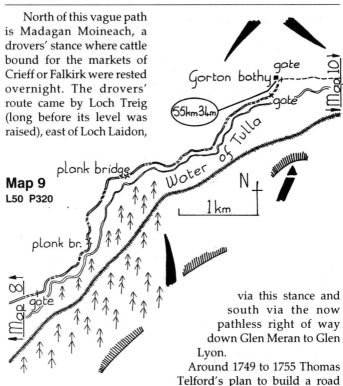

Gorton bothy
gate
gate
Map 10
55km34m
Water of Tulla
Map 9
L50 P320
plank bridge
N
1 km
plank br.
Map 8
gate

via this stance and south via the now pathless right of way down Glen Meran to Glen Lyon.

Around 1749 to 1755 Thomas Telford's plan to build a road along this route never materialised. How different today's maps would have looked with the (much later) railway following a possible second road across Rannoch Moor from north to south. Indeed would the (now) A82 ever have been built?

MAP 10. ROWANTREE COTTAGE

South of Madagan Moineach and 1km (half a mile) east of Rowantree Cottage lies Gorton Crossing. Built in the early days of the railway to cope with increasing traffic the crossing allowed trains to pass on the long stretch of single line from Bridge of Orchy to Rannoch. The crossing was manned and had a signal box. What a remote place to work in winter!

34

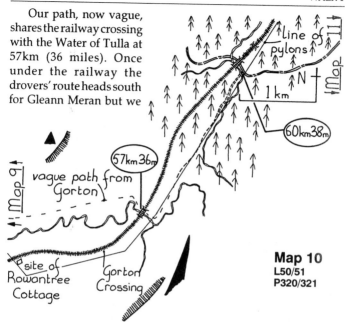

Our path, now vague, shares the railway crossing with the Water of Tulla at 57km (36 miles). Once under the railway the drovers' route heads south for Gleann Meran but we

Line of pylons

N

1 km

60km 38m

57km 36m

vague path from Gorton

Map 9

Map 11

site of Rowantree Cottage

Gorton Crossing

Map 10
L50/51
P320/321

head north-east. The pylons serve as a navigational aid and the vague path materializes into a rough track before crossing a ford and emerging at 60km (38 miles) at a forest road.

To the left the track ducks back under the railway and is often submerged as, now past the watershed, the Abhainn Duibhe flows north. We turn right to head east and north for Gleann Chomraidh and Bridge of Gaur.

MAP 11. RANNOCH FOREST

Care is needed in this, the western end of Rannoch Forest as visibility is limited to the next tree and there are some long dead-ends in the forest roads to catch the unwary! A compass is useful.

After the gate, at 64km (40 miles), a path leads off on the left to the Soldiers' Trenches. These were dug prior to the 1745 Jacobite Rebellion as practice for the Crown troops. Over 100 years before the railway these were adjacent to the drove route described previously.

About 400m after the path the right of way turns right and crosses the Duibhe Bheag by a large ford. Non-swimmers will prefer to continue straight ahead turning right, just after the gate at 65km (40.5 miles) to

Map 11
L51 P307

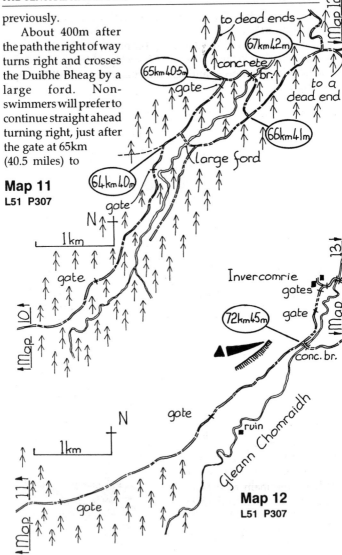

cross by the bridge. The right of way is rejoined at the left turn at 66km (41 miles).

Take care not to turn left at 67km (42 miles) and be sure to take the left-hand fork 200m further on. After 500m a high gate, at the far side of which is new planting, confirms you took all the right turnings.

MAP 12. GLEANN CHOMRAIDH

The long tramp down Gleann Chomraidh continues to the junction at 72km (45 miles) where the track over the bridge on the right is by-passed and the main track is followed out to the public road at Bridge of Gaur.

MAP 13. BRIDGE OF GAUR

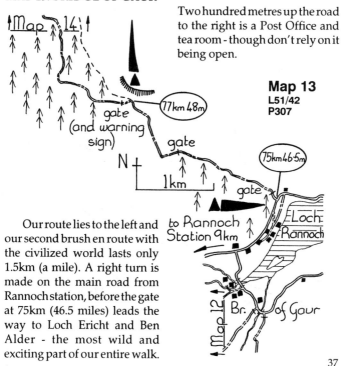

Two hundred metres up the road to the right is a Post Office and tea room - though don't rely on it being open.

Map 13
L51/42
P307

Our route lies to the left and our second brush en route with the civilized world lasts only 1.5km (a mile). A right turn is made on the main road from Rannoch station, before the gate at 75km (46.5 miles) leads the way to Loch Ericht and Ben Alder - the most wild and exciting part of our entire walk.

37

This route is shown on Roy's map of 1755.

About 100m before the second wood, at 77m (48 miles), the right of way skirts round the eastern edge of the wood, leaving the track among the trees.

MAP 14. BRIDGE OF GAUR TO LOCH ERICHT

The track through the wood is rejoined by the right of way and deteriorates as it heads north to the Cam Chriochan crossing at 84km (52 miles). The track degenerates into a maze of boggy paths as various attempts have been made to avoid the mire. We are joined here by a rough track leading from Ericht dam.

Loch Ericht is part of a major hydro-electric scheme with a dam at each end. Water is brought from as far afield as Loch Cuaich, east of Dalwhinnie, via a huge aqueduct.

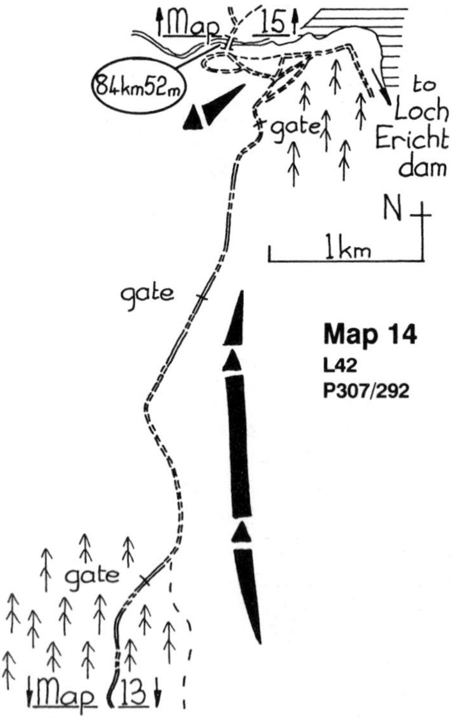

Once over the bridge keep right.

MAP 15. BENALDER COTTAGE

The footpath, which peters out altogether after a few kilometres, firstly runs close to the shore, then about 250m 'inland'. The boggy tracks running due north end on the moor leaving a very rough 1.5km to Benalder Cottage at 88km (54.5 miles).

As the path is lost, aim for the bridge across the Alder Burn. The path is again vague and rough between bridge and bothy.

Map 14
L42
P307/292

Benalder Cottage

Benalder Cottage is allegedly haunted. I have never met the ghost personally - but I have yet to spend a night there!

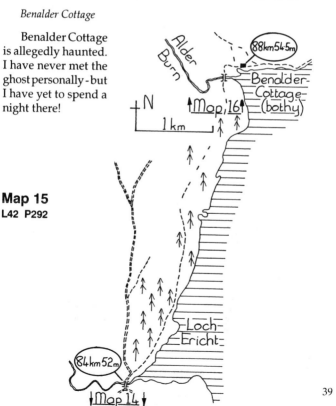

Alder Burn

88km 54.5m

Benalder Cottage (bothy)

N

↑ Map 16 ↑

1 km

Loch Ericht

Map 15
L42 P292

84km 52m

↓ Map 14 ↓

39

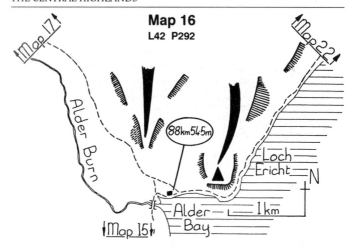

Map 16
L42 P292

88km54.5m

Loch Ericht

N

Alder Bay

1km

Map 17

Map 22

Map 15

Alder Burn

WALK 16. ALDER BURN AND LOCH ERICHT

Having survived the ghost of Benalder Cottage (or not?) the way ahead divides. Weather permitting, the excellent pony track over Bealach Cumhann and Bealach Dubh at 95km (59 miles) is the best. This also gives the option of returning to Fort William by Strath Ossian or out by the River Pattack. This route is, surprisingly, also

Rowan near Benalder Cottage - natural Bonsai?

better under foot than the first half of the alternative, the endless slog alongside Loch Ericht. However, Loch Ericht is included as an 'escape' route as it stays at a lower level.

On leaving the Cottage it is important to gain a little height, towards Prince Charlie's cave, to pick up the pony track.

MAP 17. BEALACH DUBH

Once through Bealach Cumhann and whilst marvelling at the handiwork of the path builder, we look down onto Loch Ossian. For Loch Ossian continue through the Bealach following the path right about a third of the way to Bealach Dubh, then drop directly down to the Uisge Labhair to pick up the path to Corrour Shooting Lodge. This involves a pathless kilometre (half mile) which is not much fun

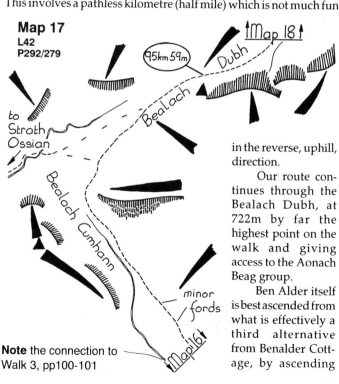

Map 17
L42
P292/279

95km 59m

Bealach Dubh

Map 18

to Stroth Ossian

Bealach

Bealach Cumhann

minor fords

Map 16

Note the connection to Walk 3, pp100-101

in the reverse, uphill, direction.

Our route continues through the Bealach Dubh, at 722m by far the highest point on the walk and giving access to the Aonach Beag group.

Ben Alder itself is best ascended from what is effectively a third alternative from Benalder Cottage, by ascending

41

Culra

past Prince Charlie's cave to Bealach Breabag between Ben Alder and Beinn Bheoil, thence picking up the path around the east side of Loch a Bhealaich Bheithe to Culra.

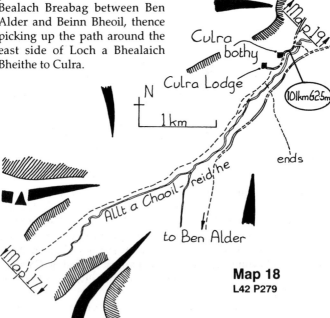

Map 18
L42 P279

42

Footbridge near Culra Bothy

MAP 18. CULRA GLEN

The descent from Bealach Dubh to Culra is plain sailing, and the path has recently been repaired. At the time of writing Ben Alder Estate still uses ponies to carry the culled deer and the path needs to be kept up.

The Ben Alder path runs into a new track at the far side of the burn to join us at a footbridge just below Culra at 101km (62.5 miles).

MAP 19. LOCH PATTACK

The route below Culra crosses the footbridge and the rough track is the right of way, although most use the better track via Loch Pattack. This better track provides access to the northern hills of the Aonach Beag group, Lochan na h-Earba and the picturesque River Pattack.

Both the good track and the right of way converge at the Pattack Iron Shed at 105km (65 miles). The 1km (half mile) section of right of way path beyond here (west) is not worth following. Cars are sometimes left at the shed (by permission) for hillwalkers heading for Ben Alder.

It is usually impossible to avoid the attention of the ponies who will search your pockets and rucksack for food however much you

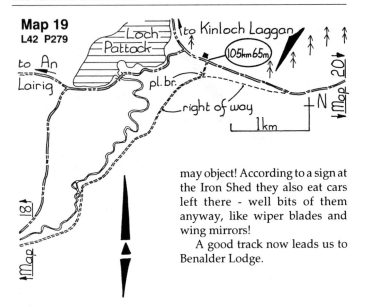

may object! According to a sign at the Iron Shed they also eat cars left there - well bits of them anyway, like wiper blades and wing mirrors!

A good track now leads us to Benalder Lodge.

MAP 20. BEN ALDER LODGE

As Benalder Lodge is approached at 107km (66 miles) the high-level track from the River Pattack joins us on our left and we by-pass the turning on the right to the estate outbuildings. The main lochside track is joined and here commences the final, level 10km (6 mile) trudge alongside Loch Ericht to Dalwhinnie.

Although there is little of interest, the walk is pleasant and we can now bask in the satisfaction of having completed the walk.

MAP 21. DALWHINNIE

This is it! Dalwhinnie at 117km (72.5 miles) is at last reached.

Dalwhinnie, 300m above sea level, has a frontier feel to it. Once a drovers' stance, Dalwhinnie was put on the map in 1728-1730 when General Wade built the new road over Drumochter and later when the railway was built. The road has been gradually realigned and upgraded - the new A9 now by-passes Dalwhinnie - once again leaving the village to fend for itself.

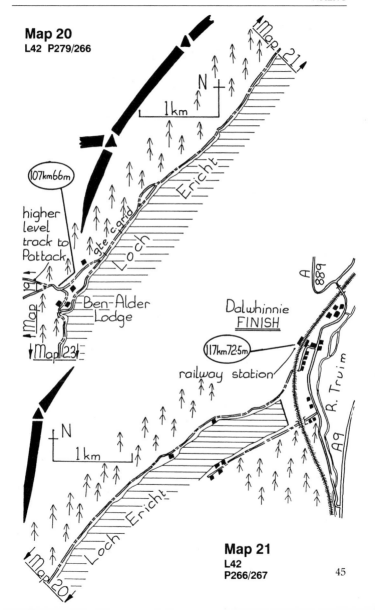

Map 20
L42 P279/266

N

1km

107km66m

higher
level
track to
Pattack

Ben-Alder
Lodge

Map 19

Map 23

Loch Ericht

Gate c and

N

1km

Dalwhinnie
FINISH

117km725m

railway station

A889

A9

R. Truim

Map 21
L42
P266/267

Map 20

Loch Ericht

45

Dalwhinnie hasn't much to offer, but with a distillery, an hotel and a railway station who needs more? A night here will allow time for reflection on the last few days, before the trip home and a return to 'civilization'. My idea of the civilized world is Loch Etive, Ben Starav, Gorton, Ben Alder, Culra, Aonach Beag....

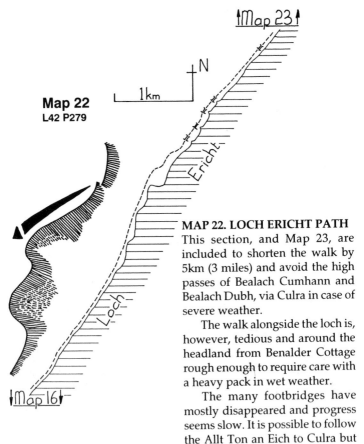

Map 22
L42 P279

MAP 22. LOCH ERICHT PATH

This section, and Map 23, are included to shorten the walk by 5km (3 miles) and avoid the high passes of Bealach Cumhann and Bealach Dubh, via Culra in case of severe weather.

The walk alongside the loch is, however, tedious and around the headland from Benalder Cottage rough enough to require care with a heavy pack in wet weather.

The many footbridges have mostly disappeared and progress seems slow. It is possible to follow the Allt Ton an Eich to Culra but this involves about 3.5km (just over 2 miles) of pathless moor.

MAP 23. LOCH ERICHT TRACK

It is with relief that, after yet another ford, the good lochside track is reached as the route continues to Ben Alder Lodge where we are joined by the track from Culra and Loch Pattack.

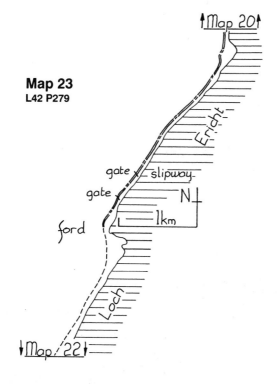

Map 23
L42 P279

47

WALK 2:
Blair Atholl to Aviemore or Tomintoul

Either of the two alternatives of this walk covers the full length of Glen Tilt, often described as the most beautiful glen in Scotland. For me the beauty of the Scottish glens lies in their variety and individual character but I would not dare argue that Glen Tilt does not rate with the best.

I suggest a south to north direction as the state of the Geldie Burn may have a bearing upon which way to go on Map 6 - it needs crossing for either route but the intrepid walker may wish to delay the decision as to which way he or she wants to walk on the wrong side of the river! All is explained later.

The Tomintoul leg of the walk touches the Linn of Dee, explores the north bank of the Dee as far as Invercauld, then strikes north over the wilds of Culardoch and Glen Builg before emerging into the green of the lower reaches of Glen Avon.

The Glen Feshie alternative crosses the wild Geldie to Feshie

Gaw's Bridge

48

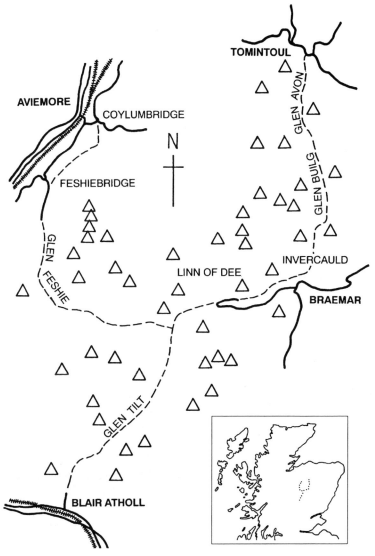

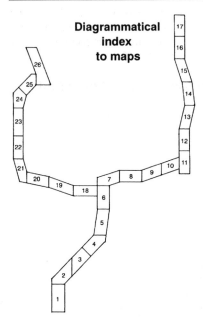

**Diagrammatical
index
to maps**

watershed, giving access to the remote An Sgarsoch and its neighbour, also Beinn Bhrotain to the north of the watershed. Glen Feshie is unique as the Feshie meanders through the ancient pines. (Efforts are now being made to encourage re-generation of our native trees - well done - but it's the deer numbers that need reducing!) The final stage of the walk is through woodland by Loch an Eilein to Aviemore.

Accommodation is limited to Inverey Youth Hostel, a few kilometres off the route, and the Feshie Bothy - very busy - so a tent is needed.

Gradient profile: Blair Atholl to Aviemore or Tomintoul

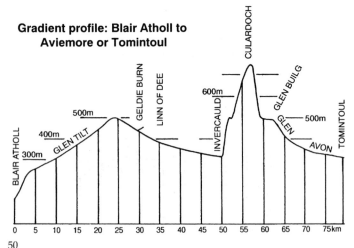

Public roads are encountered at Achlean in Glen Feshie, and from Linn of Dee to Linn of Quoich. All the remainder of the walk is on good tracks or path apart from an indistinct section from the boundary stone to Eidart Bridge on Map 19.

Walk 2: Blair Atholl to Aviemore or Tomintoul - at a glance guide

Length:	79km (49 miles) to Tomintoul. 3-5 days
	76km (47 miles) to Aviemore. 3-5 days
Total climbing:	approximately
	to Tomintoul 850m
	to Aviemore 550m
Accommodation:	Wild camping and Youth Hostel at Inverey
Roads at:	Tomintoul leg:
	Blair Atholl 0km
	Linn of Dee 36km (22 miles) to
	Linn of Quoich 42km (26 miles)
	Tomintoul 79km (49 miles)
	Aviemore leg:
	Blair Atholl 0km
	Achlean 53km (33 miles) to
	Feshiebridge 6lkm (38 miles)
	Coylumbridge 72.5km (45 miles) to
	Aviemore 76km (47 miles)
Bus services at:	Blair Atholl 0km
	Braemar (3km or 2 miles off the route)
	Tomintoul 79km (49 miles)
	Aviemore 76km (47 miles)

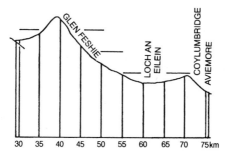

Rail services at: Blair Atholl 0km
                         Aviemore 76km (47 miles)

Access to mountain groups en route:
                         Carn Liath and Beinn a'Ghlo
                         Aviemore 'leg':
                         An Sgarsoch and Carn an Fhidhleir
                         Beinn Bhrotain and Monadh Mor
                         Mullach Clach a' Bhlair
                         Tomintoul 'leg':
                         Beinn a Bhuird
                         Culardoch

O.S. maps (in their order of appearance):
                         Landranger 43, 35 (Aviemore only), 36
                         Pathfinder 294, 281, 268, 269
                         For Tomintoul: 255, 242, 226
                         For Aviemore: 254, 241, 225 (or Outdoor Leisure 3)

MAP 1. BLAIR ATHOLL

Starting from Blair Atholl railway station head east for 1km (half a mile) and across the Bridge of Tilt. This is the old A9, now the B8079; no longer is the drive to Inverness a pleasant meander through the villages but a quick dash up the new road.

After the bridge we turn left and immediately enter Glen Tilt. The complex array of roads, tracks and paths give access to Glen Tilt, Glen Banvie and Glen Fender. There are no less than four ways to approach Glen Tilt! From the west:

1) Cross the Old Bridge of Tilt at 1.5km (1 mile) to Old Blair, turn right (north) and follow the map to reach (and cross) the Tilt at Gilbert's Bridge at 6km (4 miles) - on map 2.

2) Cross the Old Bridge of Tilt to East Lodge, turn right (north) and head up the main glen track past the east end of Gilbert's Bridge. A rough track links this to 1) above.

3) Continue past Old Bridge of Tilt to Fenderbridge and bear left over Fenderbridge, immediately at the far side of which the right of way starts. However, this now appears to intrude on private property so it is better to continue to:

4) The 'crossroads' 300m above Fenderbridge turning left past Kincraigie.

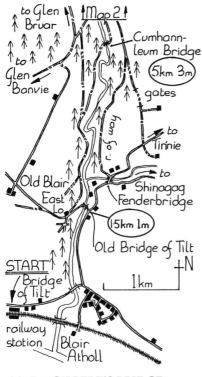

Note:

a) Routes 3 and 4 join before reaching the main glen track at Auchgobhal.

b) Route 2, though not a right of way, seems the simplest, saves wasted climbing, and is tolerated by the Estate.

Map 1
L43
P294

MAP 2. GILBERT'S BRIDGE

Thankfully, all routes join before Marble Lodge and proceed up the glen via Gaws Bridge at 9km (6 miles).

Glen Tilt was never a well-used cattle drovers' route nor did it have a military road, both due, at least in part, to the narrowness of the upper Glen. Possibly the difficult Tarf crossing was another factor.

There was, however, a plan for a railway in Glen Tilt! The Deeside line originally bound for Braemar terminated at Ballater. Future plans in the 1860s were to extend the line beyond Braemar to Blair Atholl, with a further possible line via Glen Feshie, Kingussie and Laggan to Fort William, so completing an east-west Aberdeen to Fort William line. How different our maps would look - imagine a railway junction at Geldie bothy!

The track proceeds past Balaneasie; neither the bridge on the O.S. 1:50,000 map nor the aerial ropeway marked on the O.S. 1:25,000 map still exist.

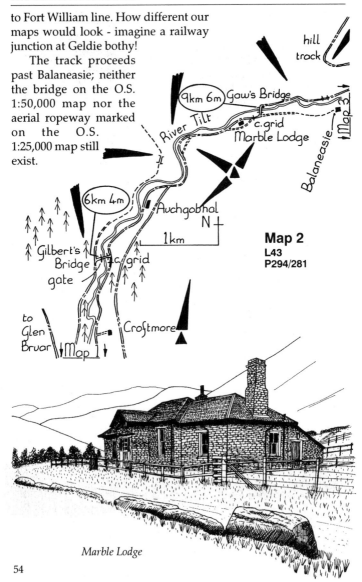

hill track

9km 6m Gaw's Bridge

River Tilt

c.grid
Marble Lodge

Balaneasie Map 3

6km 4m

Auchgobhal

N

1km

Map 2
L43
P294/281

Gilbert's
Bridge
gate

c.grid

to
Glen
Bruar Map 1

Croftmore

Marble Lodge

MAP 3. FOREST LODGE

At Clachglas (11km/7 miles) a hill
track leads north, zigzagging out
of the glen and providing a route
to Carn a' Chlamain, and
north to the remote 'Tarf
Hotel' bothy amid some
of the wildest scenery
in Scotland.

We proceed
past Forest
Lodge at

13km (8 miles).
After the second
gate the remains of
a substantial bridge
can be seen over the Tilt as
the glen narrows beneath Creag a
Chrochaidh. Here the glen continues
its characteristic water-worn 'V'
shape as distinct from the 'U' shape
of more obviously glaciated glens.

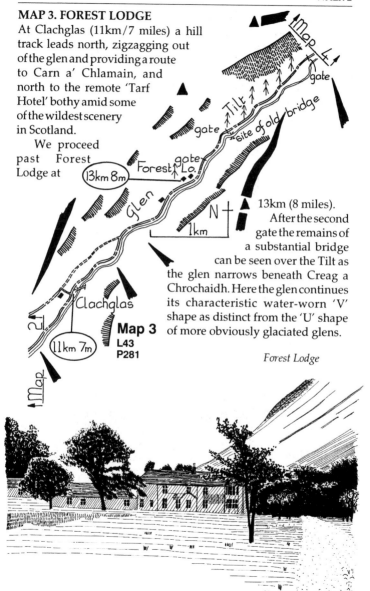

Forest Lodge

MAP 4. UPPER GLEN TILT

The new footbridge at 16.5km (10.5 miles) (grand job - well done!) provides another approach to Beinn a'Ghlo. Indeed this is the last chance to cross the Tilt to the south-east other than by using the ford to pick up the Gleann Fearnach path via Fealar Lodge.

The hill track at 18.5km (11.5 miles) is by-passed. This rises over the hill to the north and divides. The new track heads back west to An Sligearnach (and an ugly scar it is too) whilst the old track continues via the animal shelter and two-wire 'bridge' over the Tarf. A path then continues to the Tarf bothy.

Our track continues up the Tilt, by-passing the outflow of Loch Loch, the River Tilt barring access to both Loch Loch and Glen Loch from here.

Glen Tilt - footbridge

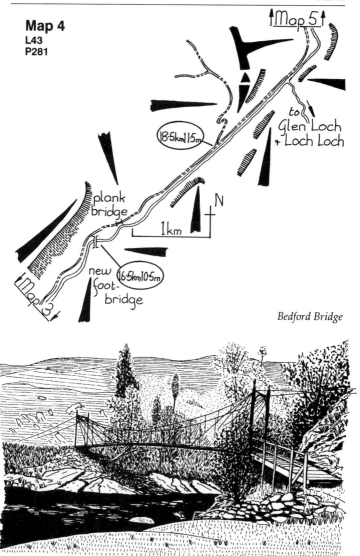

Map 4
L43
P281

↑Map 5↑

to
Glen Loch
& Loch Loch

18·5km|15m

plank
bridge

N

1km

Map 3↑

new
foot-
bridge

16·5km|10·5m

Bedford Bridge

MAP 5. BEDFORD BRIDGE

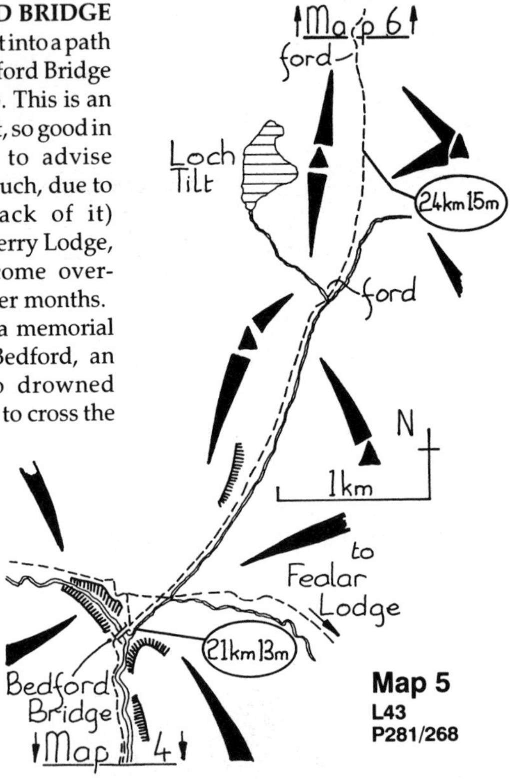

The track peters out into a path and arrives at Bedford Bridge at 21km (13 miles). This is an ideal camping spot, so good in fact that I have to advise against its use as such, due to sanitation (or lack of it) problems. As at Derry Lodge, the area can become over-used in the summer months.

The bridge is a memorial to Francis John Bedford, an English lad who drowned whilst attempting to cross the Tarf in 1879. Seven years later the bridge was even-tually built. Deep pools lie beneath the bridge, above is a gorge with the Falls of Tarf plun-ging downwards, whilst below the bridge the Tarf immediately enters the Tilt. The prospect of crossing without the bridge would be daunting indeed. Queen Victoria crossed on horseback while her pipers waded through ahead - still playing!

Once over the bridge we arrive at a crossroads of paths. Left is the very rough path which follows the north bank of the Tarf, past the far end of the two-wire bridge to the Tarf bothy, so avoiding either wading or a very precarious crossing. Right, across the now smaller River Tilt at a ford, is the right of way to Fealar Lodge, Glen Fearnach and Strath Ardle.

Our path, however, is straight ahead to cross the infant River Tilt

Bynack Lodge

at a ford, below the unseen and little known Loch Tilt.

Soon after the watershed is crossed at 24km (15 miles) at a height of about 505m.

Geldie Bothy

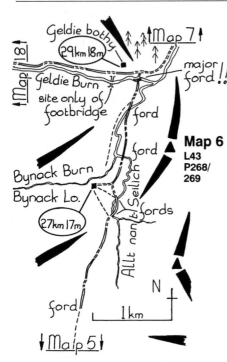

MAP 6. GELDIE FORD

The sad ruin of Bynack Lodge is reached at 27km (17 miles). At this point the condition of the rivers should be carefully noted.

The Geldie Burn is a major river and it can be impossible and dangerous to attempt a crossing opposite the Geldie bothy at 29km (18 miles). There is no bridge as shown on older maps. Depending on whether your route is via the Geldie/Feshie watershed or to Linn of Dee will govern which side of the Allt nan t-Seilich to follow.

If it is in flood the Geldie will be impassable, so to head east, keep to the east bank and stay east of the Geldie, and south of the Dee to Linn of Dee. Note there is no bridge across the Geldie Burn opposite White Bridge either!

If you are heading west to the Feshie stay south of the Geldie Burn and you may be able to cross below Geldie Lodge. If you still cannot cross, follow the track past Geldie Lodge to GR 925857, then north, past the site of Black Bothy to cross the upper Geldie, rejoining the path about 1.5km (a mile) before the Eidart Bridge.

Your troubles may not be over as the Allt Coire Bhlair crossing at GR 887890 can also be a problem. Refer to maps 18-20 pp72-74.

Above all don't take risks - and keep this book in a polythene bag!

The Geldie bothy at 29km (18 miles), assuming you have crossed the Geldie ford, is a windowless ruin possibly soon roofless as the weather takes its toll.

Continue on map 7 for Tomintoul and map 18, p72, for Aviemore.

MAP 7. WHITE BRIDGE

Having survived the ford the ruin of Ruigh nan Clach is passed. This was a summer shieling and later a bothy - now a total ruin, but when I last visited, the rhubarb in what was the garden was still growing!

The rough track soon arrives at White Bridge at 31km (19.5 miles). Just before the bridge the track on the left leads up the south-west bank of the Dee to a dead end. Over the bridge the paths on the left (which divide and rejoin) are the rights of way to Corrour, the Lairig Ghru and the central and western Cairngorm mountains.

Unlike Glen Tilt, both the Feshie/Geldie route and the Lairig Ghru were well-used drove roads. Indeed the Lairig Ghru path used to be cleared of boulders annually to enable safe passage for the beasts.

There have been numerous plans for a road over the Feshie/Geldie watershed - since General Wade's era around 1730 until comparatively recent times. Such a road would destroy what is our largest area of wilderness by dividing it in two.

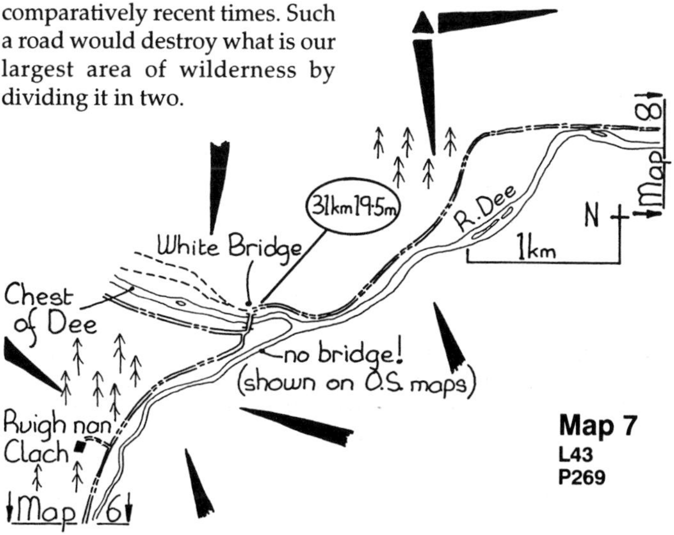

31km 19.5m

White Bridge

Chest of Dee

R. Dee

Map 18

N

1km

←no bridge!
(shown on O.S. maps)

Ruigh nan Clach

Map 16

Map 7
L43
P269

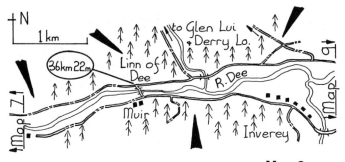

Map 8
L43 P269

MAP 8. LINN OF DEE

The improving track arrives at Linn of Dee at 36km (22 miles). This is a popular beauty spot with tourists from Braemar milling around.

Here lies a choice. To continue along the north bank of the Dee or succumb to the somewhat spartan comforts of Inverey Youth Hostel. To stay at the Hostel may be to divide up the walk by contact with civilization, or it may be a welcome break, depending on your viewpoint.

From Linn of Dee there follows 5km (3.5 miles) of road walking, by-passing the turnings to Glen Lui, Derry Lodge, the Lairig Ghru and Lairig an Laoigh; paths and tracks leading into the heart of the Cairngorms.

The Lairig Ghru suffers from over-use, as Loch Avon suffers from the easy accessibility provided by the Cairngorm chairlift. The very existence of the chairlift destroys the remoteness of Loch Avon, even though it cannot be seen.

MAP 9. LINN OF QUOICH

At 41km (25.5 miles) it is worth diverting left to walk via the Linn of Quoich, now a new bridge has been erected. Set in superb woodland the falls can be spectacular in flood. Alternatively the road can be followed to the long plank bridge at 42km (26 miles), beyond which the public road ends, to become a track from Allanaquoich.

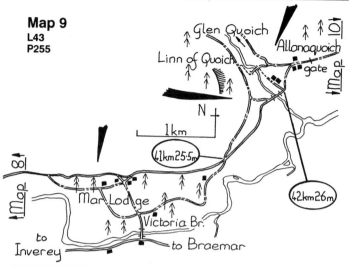

Map 9
L43
P255

Glen Quoich

Allanaquoich

gate

Linn of Quoich

N

1 km

41km 25·5m

42km 26m

Map 8

Mar Lodge

Victoria Br.

to Inverey

to Braemar

MAP 10. BALNAGOWER COTTAGE

The track continues north of the Dee, past sadly empty cottages. It is indeed a pity that no use can be found for houses that, until fairly recently were perfectly fit for habitation.

The going is easy on level tracks, passing the confluence of Clunie Water as it joins the Dee

Gleann an t-Slugain

Balnagower Cottage

Inverchand -lick Cott.

R. Dee

N

1 km

gate

Allanmore

Clunie Water

Map 10
L43
P255

BRAEMAR

River Dee

Map 9

Map 11

after crashing its way in spectacular rapids and falls through the centre of Braemar.

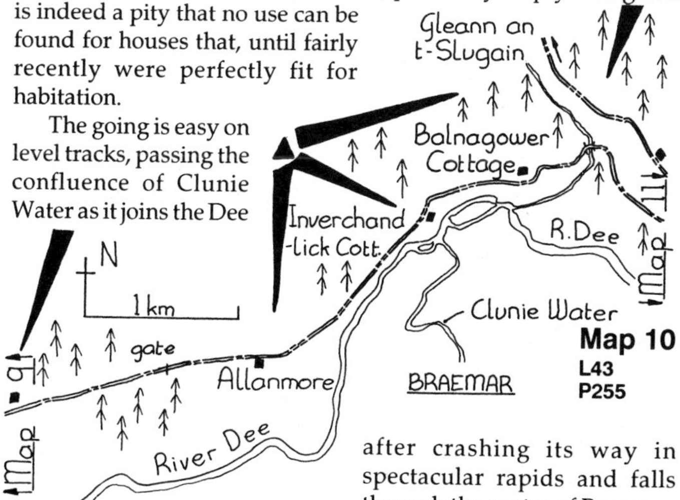

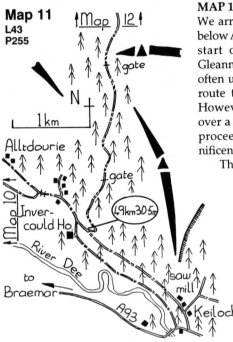

Map 11
L43
P255

↑Map↑ 12 ↑

N

1 km

Alltdourie

gate

gate

49km 30.5m

Map 10

Inver-
could Ho.

River Dee

to
Braemar

A93

saw
mill

Keiloch

MAP 11. INVERCAULD

We arrive at a 'T' junction below Alltdourie. This is the start of the very rough Gleann an t-Slugain track, often used as an approach route to Beinn a' Bhuird. However, we turn right, over a planked bridge and proceed above the magnificent Invercauld House.

The drive down to the house is private so we proceed by the left fork on the right of way. This eventually leads out to the A93 by the sawmill at Keiloch.

At 49km (30.5 miles) we turn left up through the woods, picking up the route of the old drove road past Culardoch.

This route was used to bring cattle from the north through Glen Avon, via Braemar, then via Glen Gelder or the White Mounth to Loch Muick and the Mounth Road, eventually to markets at Crieff or Falkirk.

We follow this ancient route north through woodland to a watershed.

MAP 12. CULARDOCH

The scene changes dramatically as the watershed is crossed. Woodland gives way to open moor as the track hugs the hillside, passing the junction of the Glen Feardar track at 53km (33 miles).

Glen Feardar is a glen that died. There are many abandoned

Bedford Bridge, Glen Tilt

Linn of Avon (Walk 2)
Loch Morlich (Walk 2)

farms and Queen Victoria's shieling at Auchtavan is worthy of note.

Our route climbs yet again to the shelter at 55km (34 miles). This is not a bothy but it will keep off wind and rain. Ahead the ways divide.

The first path on the left runs down alongside the Allt na Claise Moine to Glen Cairn, crossing the same by a small footbridge.

Next left is the right of way, now almost obliterated by heather and running almost due north to the Gairn. Only the purist right of way explorer with strong gaiters will want to trace this one out!

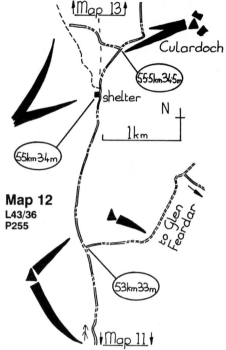

Map 12
L43/36
P255

A further short track runs to the left from reference point 55.5km (34.5 miles) and this should be ignored.

Continue up the track over the western shoulder of Culardoch.

Culardoch Shelter

A diversion of 800m to the top for the view is well worth the exertion - from the 90 degree bend in the track. This is the highest point of the track at about 728m. Culardoch is only 14m short of Munro status.

MAP 13. RIVER GAIRN

A steady descent brings us down to the River Gairn at 58km (36 miles) at which point the route of the 'official' right of way rejoins us from the left. The Gairn is bridged at 59.5km (37 miles) at which point another right of way, from Inver, joins us before we cross.

There is sadly now no shelter at Loch Builg. The Lodge fell into ruins long ago and the boathouse was demolished in 1990, shortly after a new sleeping platform had been installed.

At 60km (37 miles) we turn left, the right-hand track being yet another right of way from Glen Gairn via Corndavon Lodge.

A sharp eye should be kept for the path on the right at 61km (37.5 miles) which takes us past Loch Builg, known for both its Arctic char and eels.

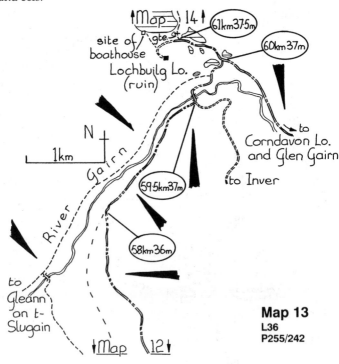

site of boathouse

Lochbuilg Lo. (ruin)

↑Map↑ 14 ↑

61km 37.5m

60km 37m

gate

N

1km

Gairn

to Corndavon Lo. and Glen Gairn

to Inver

59.5km 37m

58km 36m

River Gairn

to Gleann an t-Slugain

↓Map↓ 12 ↓

Map 13
L36
P255/242

MAP 14. GLEN BUILG

The fords in Glen Gairn shouldn't cause trouble providing you can boulder-hop with a heavy pack.

The first (small) fords at 62.5km (39 miles) should be easy, but if troublesome, stay on the east bank, over rough ground, and you will also by-pass the much larger ford 1km (half a mile) further on.

Glen Builg provides pleasant walking to arrive in Glen Avon just below the Linn of Avon. Here a new track has been built below the crags in order to avoid the final and largest of the fords. The Builg Burn is now bridged by the main Glen Avon track at 65.5km (40.5 miles).

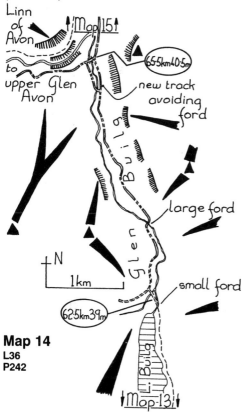

A left turn here would take us past the Pony-man's Hut and Faindouran bothy to the Fords of Avon bothy in the heart of the Cairngorms, giving access to Beinn Mheadhoin and Beinn a' Chaorainn, long mountain treks for the fit hill-walker or, in winter, a mini-expedition.

We head north.

Map 14
L36
P242

Linn of Avon

MAP 15. INCHRORY

Soon after leaving the great bend in Glen Avon we arrive at Inchrory, a magnificent lodge set in a superb location, at 66.5km (41 miles).

From Inchrory a right turn heads over a watershed only 1km (half a mile) from the Avon, to follow the River Don, virtually from its source, past Delnadamph Lodge to Corgarff Castle and the old military roads at Strathdon. Glen Avon was only a drove route, via Culardoch to the Mounth, Falkirk and Crieff, and had no military significance.

Our progress down Glen Avon is swift along a good track, which, disappointingly for the walker, becomes a metalled road about 1km before Dalestie at 70km (43.5 miles).

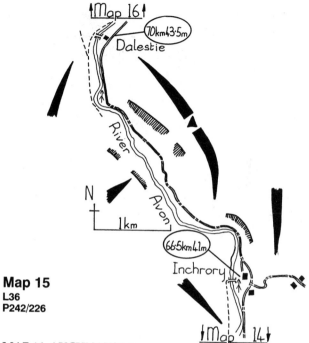

Map 15
L36
P242/226

MAP 16. AUCHNAHYLE

The metalled road continues through Torbain at 73km (45 miles) on its way to Tomintoul.

Tomintoul is reputed to be the highest village in Scotland and may have developed much further from its humble (planned) origins. Yes, Tomintoul was an early Milton Keynes of Scotland, being a planned town from the outset.

Close to Tomintoul lie large deposits of ironstone, or iron ore. A railway was planned and from 1863 to 1927 there raged a debate unique in railway history for its protracted nature. The exact route of the railway, the finance, local objections and preferences all contributed to the debate, from which the railway never materialised. Given the ironstone, the distillery and farming, as well as the passenger traffic, both Tomintoul and its railway would no doubt have prospered. However, the railway would inevitably have faced closure in the 1960s if not earlier.

Map 16
L36
P226

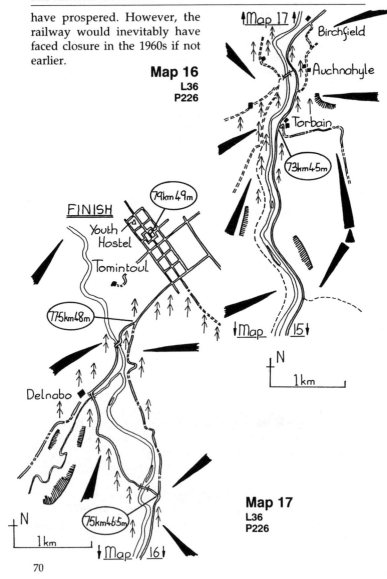

Map 17
L36
P226

MAP 17. TOMINTOUL

At 75km (46.5 miles) relief from the metalled road is at hand as it swings left to Delnabo and a track, which we take, runs straight ahead, clinging to cliffs above the River Avon.

A visit to Queen's Cairn gives a superb retrospective view of Glen Avon as far as Inchrory - all looks green and pleasant, the wilds of the upper Avon and Glen Builg being hidden from view.

The spectacular Water of Ailnack gorge runs out past Delnabo. This huge gorge, some 8km (5 miles) long, flows from The Castle, a rock formation at its start where the Water of Caiplich becomes the Water of Ailnack. (This can be viewed by a simple walk from the head of Glen Loin over the watershed.) This gorge was obviously not cut out by the relatively small burn running down it. More probably, during the last Ice Age it was carved out by a huge river under the ice-sheet, thundering along under pressure beneath, and fed by, the melting ice.

Our track rejoins the metalled road again at 77.5km (48 miles) for the last 1.5km (mile) into Tomintoul.

Here, the town's facilities are welcome and hotels, B&Bs and a Youth Hostel beckon.

Geldie Lodge

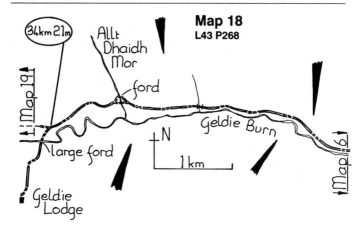

ALTERNATIVE ROUTE - Geldie Burn to Feshiebridge

MAP 18. GELDIE BURN

Assuming a successful crossing of the Geldie Burn, head almost due west along the rough track towards the Feshie/Geldie watershed. The Allt Dhaidh Mor ford can be troublesome but is nought compared with the Geldie. Continue onto the path at 34km (21 miles).

If you were unable to cross the Geldie, stay on the south bank, heading west. It may be possible to cross at the ford near the start of the path to the watershed at 34km (21 miles). If not follow the even rougher track past Geldie Lodge.

The Feshie/Geldie watershed was an important drovers' route - indeed there was pressure from 1734 to the end of the eighteenth century to build a military road connecting Ruthven Barracks with Braemar but it was never built (even though the route was surveyed by General Wade).

North of the Geldie Burn lie the heights of Beinn Bhrotain and Monadh Mor, high and remote summits to which the way is barred by mile upon mile of rough heather and peat bog. These mountains are not to be underestimated in terms of height, remoteness, and difficulty of access. Traversing the tops can require skilful navigation in mist.

MAP 19. EIDART BRIDGE

If you are north of the Geldie continue west on a clear path to the boundary cairn, after which the path becomes indistinct until the Eidart Bridge at 38.5km (24 miles).

If you are still south of the Geldie and itching to cross it don't take risks! It is better to give up! Continue past Geldie Lodge and up to the high point of the track before dropping down to the site of the old Black Bothy. Here cross the burn and head for the big bend in the Feshie (NW). You may have to go up the Geldie for a couple of hundred metres at most to find a crossing point. Once across head for Eidart Bridge - the path between the boundary stone and the bridge is too vague to find from below.

Once over the bridge the path becomes distinct.

South of this section lie the remote summits of Carn an Fhidhleir and An Sgarsoch. The cattle drovers once used the flat summit of An Sgarsoch as a cattle tryst (market), presumably for defence reasons, before the tryst was established at Crieff, and later, Falkirk.

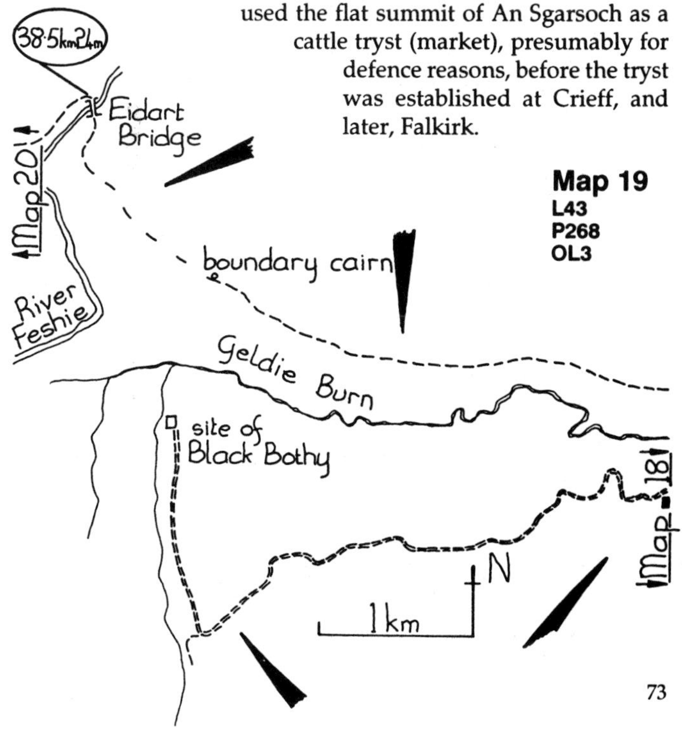

Map 19
L43
P268
OL3

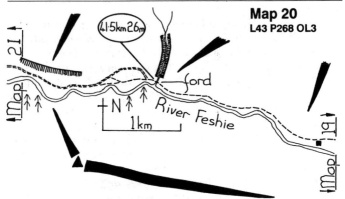

Map 20
L43 P268 OL3

41.5km 26m

ford

N

1km

River Feshie

MAP 20. ALLT COIRE BHLAIR FORD

Once across the Eidart we soon pass what is laughingly known as the Eidart Bothy. Now all that remains is the sad remnant of the wooden shed. Ten years ago I would have predicted one good storm would raze it to the ground - but it is still there. Don't rely on it for shelter.

At 41.5km (26 miles) yet another awkward ford has to be negotiated. However, an island eases the crossing and it should be possible to boulder-hop.

This point also marks the start of the Landrover track (discounting odd tracks through the heather already encountered). Save climbing by staying on the path below the track. The two rejoin after about 500m from which point the rough track is followed.

MAP 21. RUIGH AITEACHAIN

The track continues across shifting scree - in places the track has been entirely washed away and only a narrow path remains. Care is needed with a heavy pack, especially at 44km (27.5 miles).

The 'replacement' track crosses and re-crosses the Feshie and is useless for walkers for here the Feshie is a major river.

The track improves considerably as we pass 'Landseer's Chimney', a ruin where the artist is said to have stayed. We fork left at 48km (30 miles) just before Ruigh aiteachain Bothy (which now boasts a loo - of sorts!)

Keep to the left-hand track and continue down the glen.

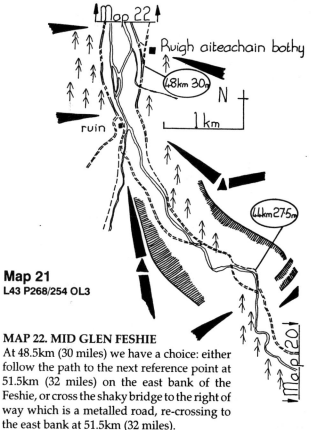

Map 21
L43 P268/254 OL3

MAP 22. MID GLEN FESHIE

At 48.5km (30 miles) we have a choice: either follow the path to the next reference point at 51.5km (32 miles) on the east bank of the Feshie, or cross the shaky bridge to the right of way which is a metalled road, re-crossing to the east bank at 51.5km (32 miles).

Note the Landrover track which arrives at the bridge at 48.5km (30 miles). This, though a terrible scar on the landscape, throws a lifeline up onto the plateau and its branches provide a valuable aid to navigation (and easy walking) if on the high plateau in mist. It is worth noting the size of the infant River Eidart at 900m. The Eidart / Einich watershed is a wild place indeed!

The path continues, east of the Feshie from reference point 51.5km (32 miles), heading north.

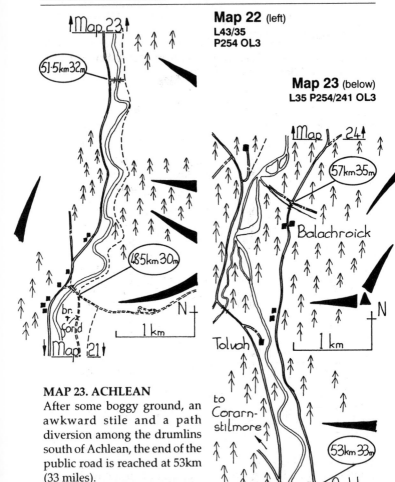

Map 22 (left)
L43/35
P254 OL3

Map 23 (below)
L35 P254/241 OL3

MAP 23. ACHLEAN

After some boggy ground, an awkward stile and a path diversion among the drumlins south of Achlean, the end of the public road is reached at 53km (33 miles).

A hundred metres from the end of the road is an unofficial car park used by hillwalkers heading for the heights that surround the remote Loch

76

Einich. Achlean is the nearest point for access - assisted by a good stalkers' path.

From Achlean there is a plod along the road to gain access to Inshriach Forest from Feshiebridge. The route is obvious, heading straight on at 57km (35 miles).

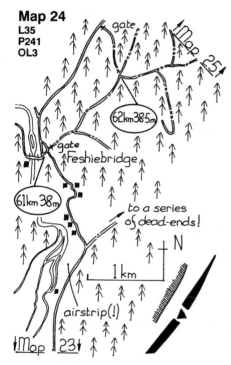

Map 24
L35
P241
OL3

MAP 24.
FESHIEBRIDGE

As we tire of this 8km (5 mile) stretch of road the boredom is relieved if the gliding club are using the airstrip. What a location for gliding! Note that there is no way through the forest without going first to Feshiebridge - all other tracks run to dead ends.

From Feshiebridge head north-east through a green (unless it has been repainted!) metal gate, fork left to reach the junction at reference point 62km (38.5 miles). From here head east, ignoring right and left branches.

MAP 25. LOCH AN EILEIN

Another left turn is by-passed and we arrive at Inshriach Bothy at 65km (40 miles). Almost immediately after this path heads north across often wet ground to pick up the path around Loch Gamhna, which in turn leads to the track around Loch an Eilein at 66.5km (41 miles).

It is possible to head north from Loch an Eilein via either Doune or Blackpark and make directly for Inverdruie and Aviemore. However, my preferred route, avoiding the visitor centre, crowds and cars, is to head east around the south shore of this beautiful lochan - noting the ruined castle on its islet - until reference point 68km (42 miles) is reached. From here turn right, heading east.

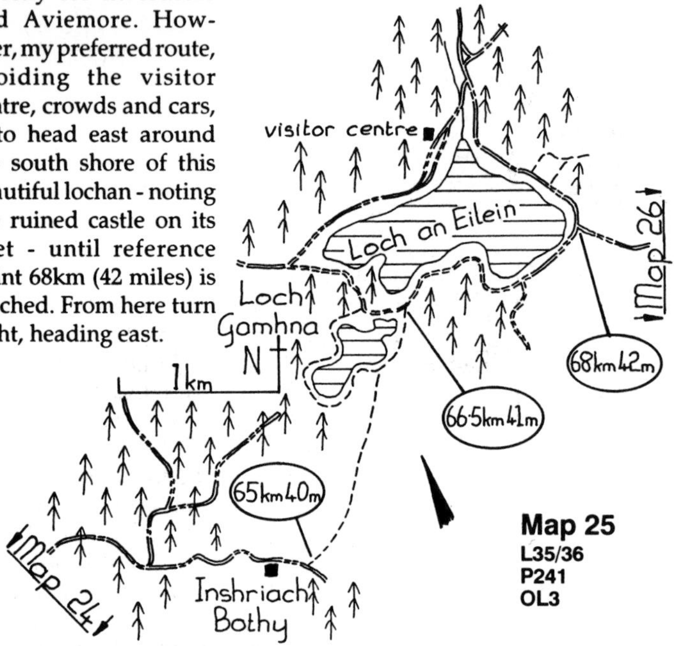

Map 25
L35/36
P241
OL3

MAP 26. AVIEMORE

We emerge on the Coylumbridge to Glen Einich track at 69.5km (43 miles) and, resisting the temptation to explore this wild and remote glen, we turn left and head north for Coylumbridge at 72.5km (45 miles).

Here start the visitor centre, gear shops, cafes and hotels! These 'facilities', I always feel, are only part-welcome after such a trek through the hills, preoccupied only with food, warmth and shelter - the basic necessities. The choice is yours, however. You can enjoy an eating-house or walk on to the station (at 76km, 47 miles), shunning the trappings of modern society!

Map 26
L36
P241/225
OL3

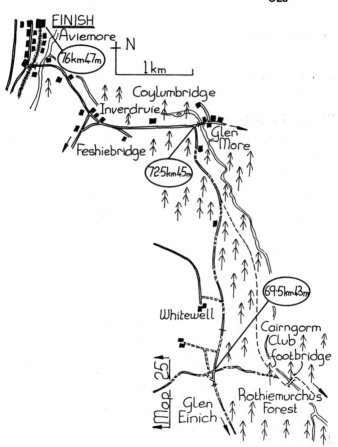

FINISH
Aviemore
N
76km47m
1km

↑ ↑ Coylumbridge
Inverdruie ↑
Glen
More
Feshiebridge ↑
72·5km45m

Whitewell
69·5km43m

Cairngorm
Club
footbridge

Map 25↑

Glen
Einich
Rothiemurchus
Forest

WALK 3:
Rannoch Moor

More a means to explore the environs of Rannoch Moor than a 'set' walk.

The main route a) takes us from Fort William, through the Nevis Gorge and on to Corrour and Rannoch before doubling back for a second crossing of the Moor to Kingshouse. Route b) provides an

Walk 3: Rannoch Moor

alternative finish by leaving the above at Loch Ossian and heading north to Tulloch. Route c) links Rannoch Moor into Walk 1 to end at Dalwhinnie.

Alternative start/finish points are given from or to d) Spean Bridge and e) and f) Kinlochleven. The Kinlochleven variations may be completed as a 'loop' from the Abhainn Rath.

At least two long walks are

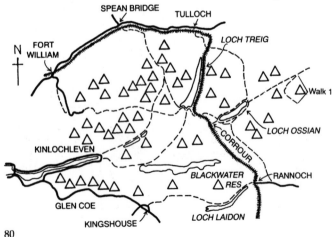

Gradient profiles: Rannoch Moor

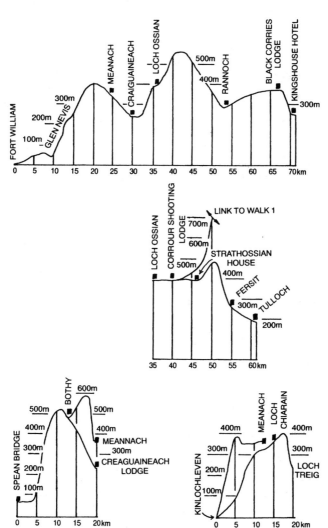

needed to fully explore the region at low level - plus additional time for days in the hills. Glen Nevis gives the best access to both the Grey Corries and the Mamores.

The routes are well surrounded by bus and rail services and Corrour and Rannoch provide mid-point transport connections. A car is an unnecessary encumbrance to be returned to. Best to leave the train and set off limited only by the number of days available.

Although there are Youth Hostels and a hotel and a bunkhouse at mid-points of the walks, self-sufficiency is again the order of the day - if only to allow time to explore the mountains en route. There are bothies at Meanach, Staoineag and Lairig Leacach and a tent allows complete freedom.

Walk 3: Rannoch Moor - at a glance guide

Length:	a)	72km (45 miles) - Fort William to Kingshouse Hotel via Rannoch. Maps 1-4 inc. 3-4 days
	b)	61km (38 miles) - Fort William to Tulloch via Strath Ossian. Maps 1-7 inc. and 15/17/18 & 19. 3 days
	c)	72km (44.5 miles) - Fort William to Dalwhinnie. Maps 1-7 inc. and 15/16. Continues on Walk 1 maps 17-21 inc. 3-5 days.

Diagrammatical index to maps

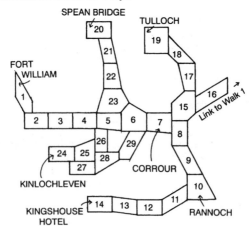

Alternative start/finishing points given to:
d)   Spean Bridge - maps 20-23 inc.
e)   Kinlochleven via Loch Eilde Mor - maps 24-26 inc.
f)   Kinlochleven via Blackwater Reservoir - maps 24
      and 27-29 inc.

Total Climbing: Refer to gradient profile

Accommodation: Youth Hostels at Glen Nevis 4km (2.5 miles) and Loch
Ossian 37km (23 miles).
Bunkhouse at Corrour 37km (23 miles) (2km off the
route)
Hotel at Rannoch
Bothies and wild camping

Roads at: Fort William 0km
Spean Bridge (alternative start/finish)
Tulloch 61km (38 miles) ('b' only)
Kinlochleven (alternative start/finish)
Rannoch 53km (33 miles) ('a' only)
Kingshouse 72km (45 miles) ('a' only)

Bus services at: Fort William 0km
Spean Bridge 0km
Tulloch 61km (38 miles)
Rannoch (post bus) 53km (33 miles)
Kinlochleven 0km
Kingshouse 72km (45 miles)

Rail services at: Fort William 0km
Spean Bridge 0km
Tulloch 61km (38 miles)
Corrour 37km (23 miles) (2km off the route)
Rannoch 53km (33 miles) (route 'a' only)

Access to mountain groups en route:
Grey Corries
Mamores

O.S. maps (in their order of appearance):
Landranger 41, 42
Pathfinder 265, 277, 278, 279, 290, 291, 292, 307, 306

MAP 1. FORT WILLIAM
a) Fort William to Kingshouse Hotel

Starting from Fort William railway station a short walk along the main road brings us to the turning for Glen Nevis, and the urban environment of Fort Bill is left behind.

I think Fort William is an opportunity wasted, from a tourism point of view. The town lies in a magnificent setting at the foot of our highest mountain, yet the planners have allowed all the worst excesses of the urban environment to develop: subways, a dual-carriageway bypass, masses of concrete, and the worst of 1970s architecture all add up to Fort William appearing to aspire to 'big city' status. With a bit of thought we could have had

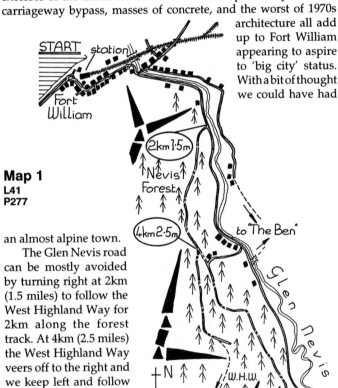

Map 1
L41
P277

an almost alpine town.

The Glen Nevis road can be mostly avoided by turning right at 2km (1.5 miles) to follow the West Highland Way for 2km along the forest track. At 4km (2.5 miles) the West Highland Way veers off to the right and we keep left and follow the forest track up the Glen.

84

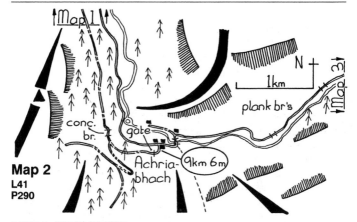

Map 2
L41
P290

MAP 2. GLEN NEVIS

Keeping left after the concrete bridge we run out of forest track and are obliged to rejoin the metalled road at Achriabhach at 9km (6 miles).

We turn right, cross the River Nevis on the road and head off up the thankfully short stretch of tarmac to the car park.

My wife and I walked Glen Nevis in the opposite direction, from Meanach bothy to Fort William station, in the type of foul conditions only Glen Nevis could conspire to throw at us and we noted there is absolutely no shelter in the 24km (15 mile) route - be warned!

MAP 3. NEVIS GORGE

At last the car park is reached at 12km (7.5 miles) and the popular path up Nevis Gorge commences. The path provides a grandstand view of the spectacular gorge and indeed this section is well used.

Quite suddenly the mood changes as the path levels out and the climbing hut with its precarious three-wire bridge is reached, below Steall waterfall.

A path climbs the side of the falls to the hanging valley, once described by a friend of mine as the only vertical bog he had climbed. The proper path climbs from a point a little further east and winds its way steeply up An Garbhanach and into the central Mamores.

Steall Bridge, Glen Nevis

I reached this point in Glen Nevis in my late 'teens when on a camping trip in the late 1960s. I remember gazing into the remoteness of the upper Glen Nevis longingly. Having neither the experience nor the equipment to undertake a cross-country hike, my friend and I turned round and returned to the car park. We scaled Ben Nevis with everyone else but the seeds were sown for the idea of

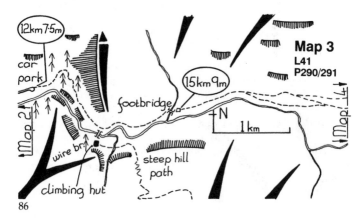

undertaking a long cross-country trek...one day!

A footbridge is reached at 15km (9 miles) where the Allt Coire Giubhsachan comes crashing down from another hanging valley, this time to the north of the main glen. The ruin of Steall is passed and the climb to the watershed begins.

The path divides. It makes no difference which is followed - both can be boggy.

MAP 4. WATER OF NEVIS

The path rejoins and the glen once again levels out.

North are the precipitous slopes of Sgurr a Bhuic (963m) forming the southern spur of Aonach Beag, a fine peak (1234m), oddly higher than Aonach Mor (1221m). The Mor (big) and Beag (little) refer to the bulk of the mountains as Aonach Mor is flat topped, unlike its higher and more shapely neighbour.

Years ago (1970) whilst on Ben Nevis I witnessed a massive rockfall on the west face of Aonach Beag. A crack like a gunshot drew our attention, by which time rocks the size of cottages were crashing down the mountain. The scar of newly severed rock was visible for years.

The watershed is marked by the strange little hillock of Tom an Eite at 20km (12.5 miles), standing guard between the rivers of both Glen Nevis and Abhainn Rath. The glen from here to the head of Loch Treig has no name. It deserves one for this glen is the centre of

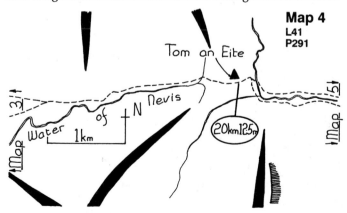

87

the routes hereabouts; the hub of the wheel.

At Tom an Eite a decision has to be made, especially if the rivers are in spate. North of the Abhainn Rath for Meanach bothy, and the two paths leading to the Lairig Leacach; or south of the Abhainn Rath for Loch Eilde Mor (and Beag) and Staoineag bothy. The right of way, and marginally better path, runs north of the river. Both paths ford tributaries of the main river.

MAP 5. MEANACH

At 24km (15 miles) yet another ford is crossed and immediately after the path on the north side is joined by the Lairig Leacach path from Glen Spean. Just east of this and still on the north side is Meanach bothy. Opposite the bothy is probably the last practical crossing point of the Abhainn Rath - a long, deep paddle, and definitely out of the question in flood.

The buildings south of the river at Luibeilt are ruinous and mark the end of the track past Loch Eilde Mor and Loch Eilde Beag, from Kinlochleven.

The two paths continue east of Meanach and Luibeilt, either side of the now uncrossable Abhainn Rath, which crashes down some rapids 1.5km (a mile) before Staoineag on its way to Loch Treig and the Fort William aluminium works hydro-electric plant.

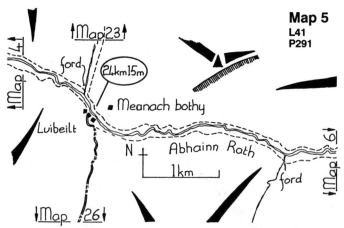

Map 5
L41
P291

Staoineag

MAP 6. LOCH TREIG

As we continue east the southern path passes by Staoineag bothy at 27km (17 miles). Meanach, Staoineag and the Lairig Leacach bothies are all maintained by the Mountain Bothies Association. Well done to all concerned - these shelters can be vital in such a region.

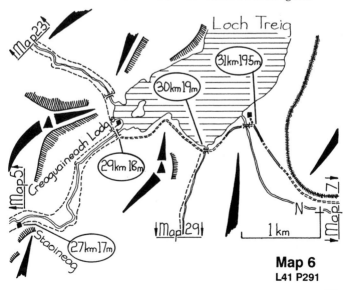

Map 6
L41 P291

Loch Treig

The paths converge at a substantial plank bridge near Creaguaineach Lodge at 29km (18 miles). Here the eastern 'leg' of the Lairig Leacach path arrives from the north. This splits in two but the path on the south-west bank of the Allt na Lairige is the right of way.

From the lodge we continue on a rough Landrover track - but how does even a Landrover get here for this 3km (2 mile) section of track serves only as a link between the several footpaths in the region. There is no vehicular track connection to anywhere else!

At 30km (19 miles) there is another substantial bridge. This lies across the outflow from Gleann Iolairean, part of the old drove road from Kinlochleven, past Blackwater dam and north by Loch Treig.

This drove route was probably disused by the time the railway was built and certainly fell into disuse as the railways took over the movement of cattle. The building of the West Highland Railway, and the raising of Loch Treig by 10.5m has virtually closed off the right of way north. Indeed, so confined is the glen that 2km (a mile) of railway line had to be realigned to allow the building of the small dam. The old alignment is still visible below the dam.

90

A right of way north heads from reference point 31km (19.5 miles) between railway and loch to GR 343724, crossing under the railway with the Allt Coire Mheadhoin. It then continues north to Fersit above the railway across the precipitous slopes of Stob Coire Sgriodain at 979m. The route has nothing to commend it and the only practical escape by Loch Treig is by rail.

The railway climbs some 80m alongside Loch Treig and our track heads south, climbing up to the side of the line.

MAP 7. CORROUR STATION
Our track passes under the railway at 33.5km (21 miles).

A rough path also continues to head south to Corrour Station, west of the railway, but the several bridges on this had all collapsed but one on my last sortie to these parts; better to stick to the right of way despite the slight climb beyond the railway.

Eventually the path becomes a track and a further path shortcuts to reference point 36km (22.5 miles). This is a major junction: north of Loch Ossian the main track runs to Strath Ossian. What a wonderful name - Ossian originates from the name of the bardic son of Fionn MacCumhail, also known as Fingal. South of Loch Ossian the right of way also runs to Strath Ossian - on a good track.

Don't assume you will get in at the hostel - once my wife and I turned up mid-afternoon, duly waited until the opening time of 5.00

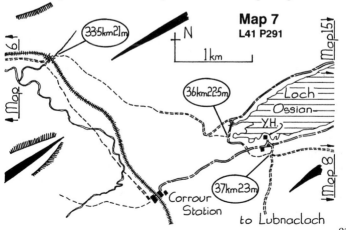

p.m. to be told every bed was booked by a school party for two weeks - solid! And we were told we couldn't camp either.

Thank goodness for Corrour Station Bunkhouse. This is a basic bunkhouse in the old station buildings - and a very pleasant evening was spent in the old signal box which gave a panoramic view of the moor while the sun set.

Here the ways divide: a) map 8 for Rannoch and Kingshouse; b) map 15 for Corrour Shooting Lodge and Tulloch; c) via part of Walk 1, for Dalwhinnie.

MAP 8. LOCH OSSIAN

Soon the path junction is reached at 39km (24 miles). Here another

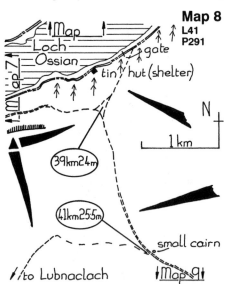

path comes up from the south side of Loch Ossian (this path is difficult to locate from the other end, and leaves the loch shore track 200m east of an old iron gate).

From the junction we head south on an improving path which eventually improves to rough track, passing a small cairn at 41km (25.5 miles) where a vague and rough path comes up the hill from Lubnaclach.

MAP 9. CORROUR OLD LODGE

At 42.5km (26 miles) the ruins of Corrour Old Lodge are reached. This was a traditional shooting lodge for many years until its use changed and the buildings were used as an isolation hospital. Isolation in every sense - at 540m on Rannoch Moor!

It is worth stopping here to gaze west at the magnificent

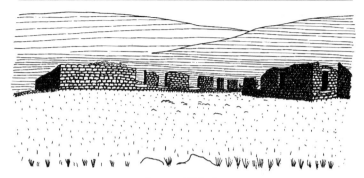

Corrour Old Lodge

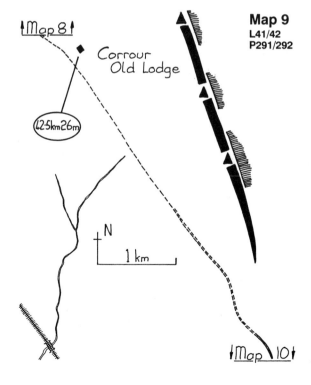

Map 9
L41/42
P291/292

↑Map 8↑

Corrour
Old Lodge

12.5km 26m

N

1 km

↓Map 10↓

93

panorama. This is in my opinion the best view of Ben Nevis. Only from the west can we see just how much higher The Ben is in comparison with its surrounding mountains. From Corrour Old Lodge Ben Nevis stands aloft behind the lesser peaks of the Mamores and the Grey Corries like a father figure with his younger family gathered round.

Speaking of mountains, behind, that is just east of Corrour Old Lodge, Carn Dearg (941m) tops a fine north-south ridge and a little further east lie Sgor Gaibhre (955m) and Sgor Choinnich (929m). These remote peaks are so close at hand it would be a shame to miss them out....

We head south to the Rannoch road, the track gradually improving - this is easy walking indeed!

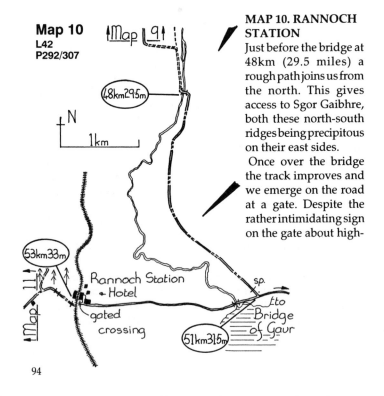

Map 10
L42
P292/307

MAP 10. RANNOCH STATION

Just before the bridge at 48km (29.5 miles) a rough path joins us from the north. This gives access to Sgor Gaibhre, both these north-south ridges being precipitous on their east sides.

Once over the bridge the track improves and we emerge on the road at a gate. Despite the rather intimidating sign on the gate about high-

The Benton Stone - Rannoch Station

velocity rifles (do these hurt more than ordinary rifles?) another signpost describes the track as 'The Road to the Isles'. We have now completed 51km (31.5 miles), plus of course any sorties into the hills which will have been hard to resist in such a superb area.

We head west to Rannoch Station at 53km (33 miles). The tea room here opens in May, which is a bit of a long wait if you turn up in November - but there is a very snug little bar in the Rannoch Hotel....

MAP 11. LOCH LAIDON

Dragging ourselves away from the Rannoch Hotel/tea room/bar/ option of a train ride home (!) we cross the railway just south of the station at the 'Stop, Look, Listen' crossing (you can hear trains for about 2 miles before they arrive at Rannoch!).

A good track leads into the woods above Loch Laidon. The right of way follows the shore, then climbs up to the line of pylons as we leave the wood but the way is rough and complicated by deer fencing.

Ignoring the first right turn it is best to follow the main track until it ends at a ford at 56km (35 miles). Cross the ford and drop steeply down the hillside for about 150m to the pylons (pylon no. 47 to be exact) then head south-west under the line of pylons.

If covering this ground in the reverse direction it is vital to identify pylon no. 47 then head up to the track as a) the track cannot

be seen from below,
b) the link is not
possible at any
other point, other
than by crawling
through the
trees, and c) to
continue the
way is barred by

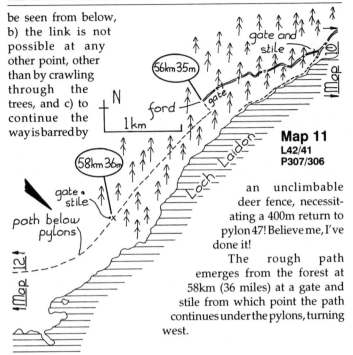

Map 11
L42/41
P307/306

an unclimbable
deer fence, necessit-
ating a 400m return to
pylon 47! Believe me, I've
done it!

The rough path
emerges from the forest at
58km (36 miles) at a gate and
stile from which point the path
continues under the pylons, turning
west.

MAP 12. MENZIE'S STONE

There isn't much on this map because there isn't much out there.
Navigation is simplified due to the man-made intrusion of the
pylons, the line of which the path slavishly follows so there is not
even the preoccupation of using the compass.

Life is simplified to the act of plodding through the nearest thing
we have to true wilderness - superb. Such a featureless landscape
makes arrival at Menzie's Stone (an unexciting boulder at 63km/
39.5 miles on what is now the Highland Region/Tayside Region
boundary) a cause for celebration - perhaps even a Mars bar!

This rock, the significance of which I have still to learn, lies just
south-east of pylon 113 - yes, the 67th we walk past. This is
identified by its pair of guy wires as the line of pylons changes its

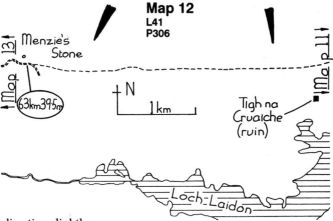

Map 12
L41
P306

Menzie's
Stone

Map 13

Map 11

63km395m

Tigh na
Cruaiche
(ruin)

+N
1 km

Loch-Laidon

direction slightly.

Here we also join the Black Corries track and can begin to enjoy the fine prospect of Buachaille Etive Mor, straight ahead for the next few kilometres and one of the reasons for ending at Kingshouse rather than starting there. Indeed, heading east from Kingshouse involves much turning round, walking backwards and stopping to admire this classic but not over-rated view of one of our finest mountains.

Map 13
L41
P306

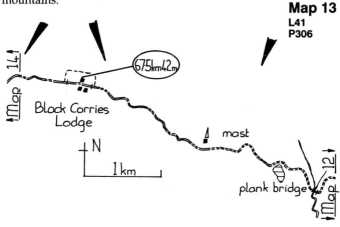

Map 14

675km42m

Map 12

Black Corries
Lodge

+N
1 km

mast

plank bridge

MAP 13. BLACK CORRIES LODGE

The rough track twists and turns across boggy terrain, improving as it passes the mast, until Black Corries Lodge is reached at 67.5km (42 miles). Here the owner has seen fit to bar access via the lodge, which in itself is fair enough as the track may be regarded as an intrusion. However, the diversion has not been made - one is expected to struggle and at times paddle around the lodge - on the north side over rough, boggy, pathless terrain. A path would be welcomed.

Back on the track we head west.

MAP 14. KINGSHOUSE HOTEL

The track descends by the Allt Chailleach which, together with the River Coupall, which flows the 'wrong' way out of Glencoe, forms the River Etive.

We emerge at a gate onto the old (1930s) main road and West Highland Way. Kingshouse Hotel, our final destination, lies 250m to our left at 72km (45 miles) from our start in Fort William.

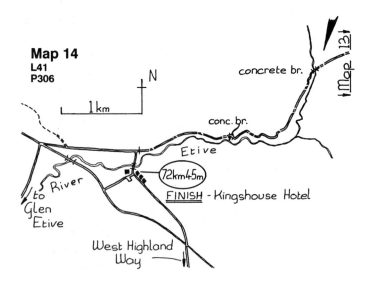

Map 14
L41
P306

N

1 km

concrete br.

Map 131

conc. br.

Etive

to River Glen Etive

72km 45m

FINISH - Kingshouse Hotel

West Highland Way

Kingshouse Hotel

b) ALTERNATIVE FINISH to Tulloch
MAP 15. CORROUR SHOOTING LODGE

This map depicts the right of way south of Loch Ossian, which is used if bound for Strath Ossian and Tulloch.

The turning to Rannoch is ignored both opposite the Youth Hostel and at 39.5km (24.5 miles). We continue to

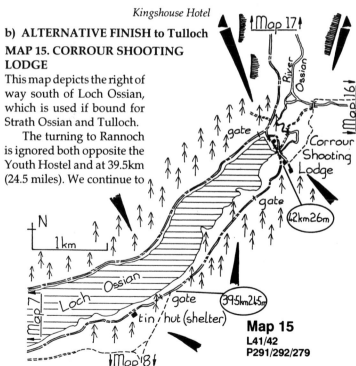

Map 15
L41/42
P291/292/279

Corrour Shooting Lodge at 42km (26 miles). After passing through the gate and trying to avoid the attention of the ponies we cross the bridge just before the Lodge.

A private drive leads into the Lodge grounds, a loop track by-passes the Lodge and is used for Strath Ossian, whilst a further

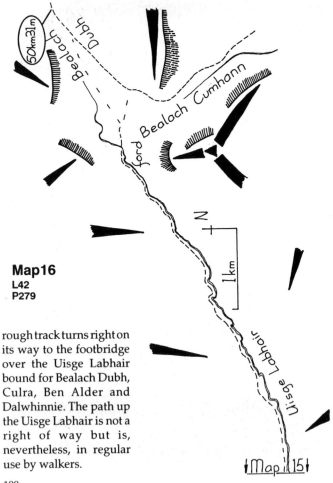

Map16
L42
P279

rough track turns right on its way to the footbridge over the Uisge Labhair bound for Bealach Dubh, Culra, Ben Alder and Dalwhinnie. The path up the Uisge Labhair is not a right of way but is, nevertheless, in regular use by walkers.

100

c) ALTERNATIVE FINISH to Dalwhinnie

MAP 16. BEN ALDER LINK

This map depicts the link to Culra only - for Strath Ossian continue on map 17 (p102).

The path up Uisge Labhair becomes faint, crosses a ford and then peters out. To head for Bealach Dubh, continue on rising ground to GR 473727 to join the Culra pony track, which avoids scrambling up a steep hillside with a heavy pack. The pony track should be gained almost a kilometre before the Bealach at 50km (31 miles).

Note this reference point equates to 95km (59 miles) on Walk 1, map 17 (p41).

If making the connection in the reverse direction, drop down from the pony track from GR 468719 to the end of the Uisge Labhair path as shown on the O.S. 1:50,000 map.

MAP 17. STRATH OSSIAN

A good track heads north through Amar Strath Ossian to Strath Ossian.

We arrive at reference point 45km (28 miles) at which point the right of way follows the direct line past Strathossian House at 46km (28.5 miles), where an open outbuilding may provide temporary shelter. Although the Allt Feith Thuill is bridged the environs of the

Strath Ossian

house are wet and at least a couple of minor fords have to be crossed.

In wet conditions, and if not seeking shelter, it may be easier to follow the new track on its longer loop west - at least height is not lost - to rejoin the old track at 47km (29 miles).

Note the faint path following Allt Feith Thuill which gives access to Stob Coire Sgriodain (979m) and Meall Garbh (976m) and Chno Dearg (1046m), east of Loch Treig.

Also, the long north-east ridge of Beinn na Lap (937m) makes it possible to include this mountain on the way to or from Corrour, the climb being partly offset by saving considerable distance.

From reference point 47km (29 miles) our route lies along the rising hill path heading due north. It is possible to follow the main track which enters the wood in 3km (2 miles) but provides a somewhat tedious walk to Fersit (or via Luiblea to Loch Laggan). The only reason to use the forest tracks will be to avoid the fords which cross our path immediately before Fersit.

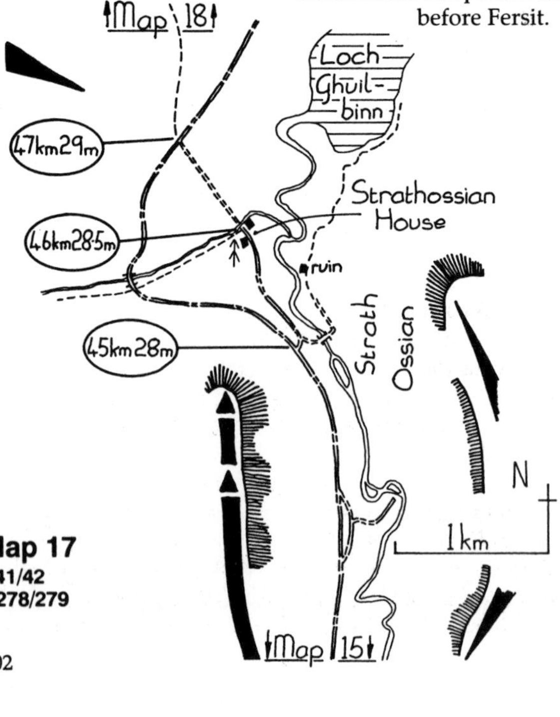

Map 17
L41/42
P278/279

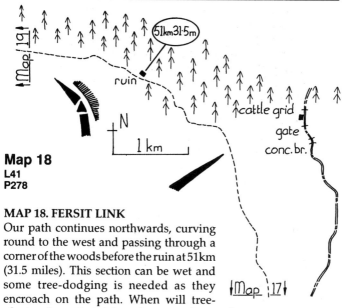

Map 18
L41
P278

MAP 18. FERSIT LINK

Our path continues northwards, curving round to the west and passing through a corner of the woods before the ruin at 51km (31.5 miles). This section can be wet and some tree-dodging is needed as they encroach on the path. When will tree-planters learn that rights of way need more than a 1m space!

The ruin provides no shelter other than as a windbreak and we continue west to the fords above Fersit.

MAP 19. TULLOCH

The path leaves the edge of the wood and arrives at the fords above Fersit. The vast northern slopes of Chno Dearg are drained by a confusion of burns that divide and rejoin to form themselves into two rivers which can be difficult to cross in spate. Fersit is so near but it's a long way back; hence the need for careful consideration at reference point 47km (29 miles).

After either boulder-hopping or paddling the track is reached and a left turn brings us to the bridges over the West Highland Railway and the River Treig at 55km (34 miles).

Note there is no direct route to Tulloch Station despite a promising-looking track heading off in that direction. The public road has to be followed to cross the River Spean at 58.5km (36 miles).

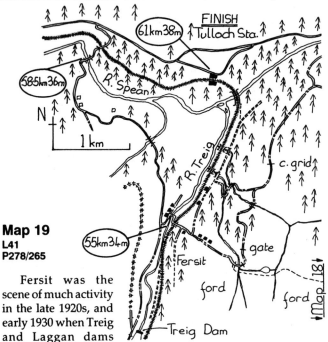

Map 19
L41
P278/265

Fersit was the scene of much activity in the late 1920s, and early 1930 when Treig and Laggan dams were built. The course of the old railway - incorrectly marked on the O.S. map as a 'disused tramway' - can be seen crossing the hillside just above Fersit. (This is also encountered on the approach to the Lairig Leacach on map 21 (p106).)

Four miles of road brings us to the end of our walk at Tulloch Station at 61km (38 miles).

If car transport is used for the pick-up it is possible to park at the end of the public road, by the start of the track to Treig Dam at GR 350782.

d) CONNECTION to Spean Bridge

MAP 20. SPEAN BRIDGE

This section describes the route from Spean Bridge to either Meanach bothy or Creaguaineach Lodge, both being a distance of 18km (11.5

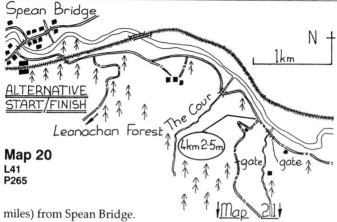

Map 20
L41
P265

miles) from Spean Bridge.

Meanach bothy appears on map 5 (p88) at reference point 24km (15 miles) and Creaguaineach Lodge appears on map 6 (p89) at 29km (18 miles), these distances being from Fort William.

The Cour is a major tributary of the River Spean, or was until much of it was diverted into the hydro scheme, and it effectively separates the eastern end of Leanachan Forest from the Lairig Leacach track. Spean Bridge station to Corriechoille has therefore to be walked on the pleasant minor road to reference point 4km (2.5 miles).

Note there is no bridge at GR 285805 - this was washed away in storms in December 1991 so don't even think about starting from Roy Bridge instead!

From reference point 4km (2.5 miles) a track zigzags southward, west of the Allt Leachdach.

MAP 21. ALLT LEACHDACH

The track to the far eastern end of Leanachan Forest is ignored and the old hydro scheme railway here is crossed at 6km (4 miles). This area was known as 'Central' during the building of the hydro scheme tunnel and this, its associated railway line. Here during the building of the hyrdo scheme there was a canteen and even a small hospital. Many men were based here with further camps for 650 at Fersit and 350 at Roughburn, near Laggan Dam. This was a huge

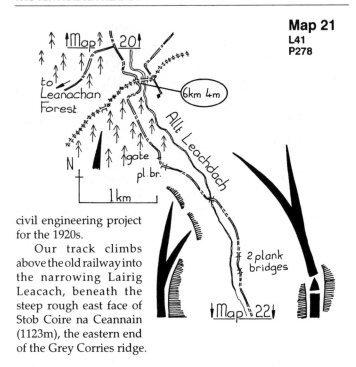

Map 21
L41
P278

6km 4m

Allt Leachdach

to Leanachan Forest

N

↑gate
pl. br.

1 km

2 plank bridges

↑Map↓ 22↓

civil engineering project for the 1920s.

Our track climbs above the old railway into the narrowing Lairig Leacach, beneath the steep rough east face of Stob Coire na Ceannain (1123m), the eastern end of the Grey Corries ridge.

MAP 22. LAIRIG LEACACH

The track passes over the watershed about 1.5km (a mile) before the Lairig Leacach bothy. About 300m before the bothy a low col in the east, 100m above the track, provides access to Stob Coire Easain (1115m) and Stob a' Choire Mheadhoin (1105m), two fine peaks west of Loch Treig, also accessible from Fersit. Indeed Coire Laire provides a pathless route from Fersit to the Lairig.

No fewer than three paths lead from the vicinity of the tiny bothy at 12.5km (8 miles) from Spean Bridge. From the west:

The path to Meanach passes over a higher watershed - this is a right of way. A ridge leads from the watershed to the odd man out on the Grey Corries ridge, Stob Ban.

The path following the south-west bank of the Allt na Lairige is

Lairig Leacach Bothy

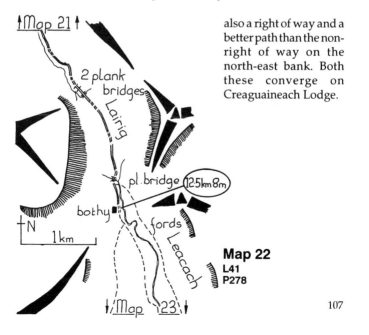

also a right of way and a better path than the non-right of way on the north-east bank. Both these converge on Creaguaineach Lodge.

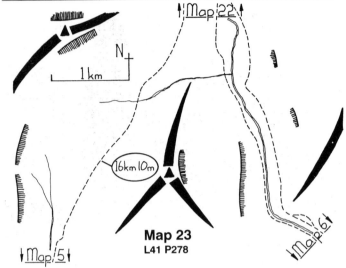

Map 23
L41 P278

MAP 23. SOUTH LAIRIG LEACACH

The three paths continue to the nameless glen drained by the Abhainn Rath. The westerly path passes over the highest point (over 580m) at 16km (10 miles) from Spean Bridge. The Lairig Leacach proper is only at about 500m.

The wet descent of the western path to Meanach contrasts with the tortuous nature of the two eastern paths as they follow the Allt na Lairige to Creaguaineach Lodge.

Refer now to the 'main' route depicted on maps 5 and 6.

e) CONNECTION to Kinlochleven via Loch Eilde Mor

MAP 24. KINLOCHLEVEN

At first glance Kinlochleven doesn't seem to have much going for it. A dull, sunless town (in winter anyway) with a closed-down aluminium works. The town is by-passed now by the Ballachulish Bridge - at least when the old ferry ran it was sometimes quicker to drive via Kinlochleven rather than queue. Now even that has gone. Kinlochleven is the poor relation of neighbouring Glen Coe. However, the West Highland Way has put some life back into the place. How wrong are first impressions! Kinlochleven is a route

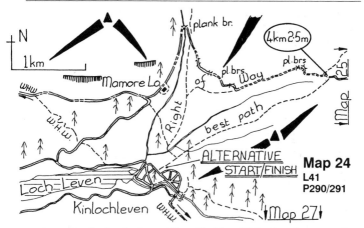

centre not only for the busy West Highland Way but for some fine ways onto the north side of Rannoch Moor. Two hundred metres out of the village a network of paths and tracks awaits.

The first of the two alternative routes onto the moor sets off through delightful woodland from the right-hand side of the church at GR 188623. A maze of paths explore the woods and falls, eventually forming the right of way and 'best path' on my map.

These eventually join together at 4km (2.5 miles) at the Lairigmor/ Mamore Lodge/Loch Eilde Mor high-level track which contours along above Kinlochleven to the north of the town. The West Highland Way, the metalled road to the Mamore Lodge Hotel and the hill track up Allt Coire na Ba (bound for the Mamores) also connect Kinlochleven to this high track.

From reference point 4km (2.5 miles) a further hill track leads by Coire an Lochain to Sgurr Eilde Mor (1010m), Binnein Mor (1130m) and Binnein Beag (943m).

Our track leads north-east to Loch Eilde Mor.

MAP 25. LOCH EILDE MOR

Soon a path turns right, also marked 4km (2.5 miles). This cross-country route, though not a right of way, links our track with the Monument to Loch Chiarain path forming either a circular walk from Kinlochleven or, as I have done, from and returning to Meanach bothy.

However, we plod on past the boathouse to reference point 5km (3 miles) where a second path rises to Coire an Lochain on our left bound for the Mamores.

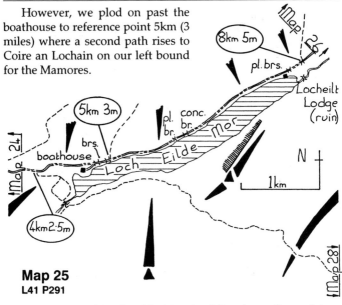

Map 25
L41 P291

The waters of Loch Eilde Mor (and Beag) are diverted into Blackwater Reservoir by a pipeline, the outflow of which can be seen at the northern end of the Blackwater Dam.

The remains of Locheilt Lodge are passed at 8km (5 miles) beyond which the northern loop of the Coire an Lochain path joins us from the left.

MAP 26. LOCH EILDE BEAG

The track continues alongside Loch Eilde Beag and crosses the watershed only 1.5km (a mile) before Abhainn Rath.

The track ends at the rather untidy collection of ruins at Luibeilt at 12km (8 miles) from Kinlochleven.

The bad news is that Meanach bothy is across the other side of the river which, if in spate, will mean a diversion left to Tom an Eite to find a crossing point (some 2.5km/1.5 miles west) or east to Staoineag which is on our side of the main river. These options should involve no more than boulder-hopping or paddling whereas

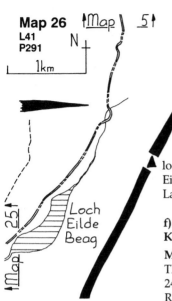

Map 26
L41
P291
N
1km

↑Map 5↑

Loch
Eilde
Beag

↑Map 25↑

↑Map 24↑

opposite Meanach is at best a long, cold, knee-deep wade!

Note that a distance of 12km (8 miles) from Kinlochleven brings us to reference point 24km (15 miles) on the route from Fort William (on map 5 p88).

Note also that Kinlochleven to Spean Bridge via Loch Eilde Mor and the western leg of the Lairig Leacach is 30km (19 miles).

f) CONNECTION to Kinlochleven via Loch Chiarain

MAP 27. RIVER LEVEN

This route leaves Kinlochleven (map 24 p109) on the north side of the River Leven (do not cross the River Leven to the obvious track at the other side of the river - this leads up by the pipelines and takes a longer and less picturesque route to the south end of Blackwater Dam).

The path immediately leads into pleasant woodland and meanders up the

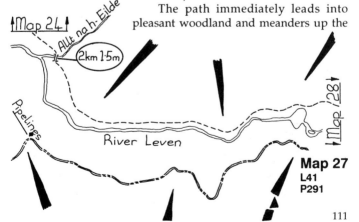

↑Map 24↑
Allt na h-Eilde
2km 1·5m
↑Map 28↑
Pipelines
River Leven

Map 27
L41
P291

north bank of the River Leven, crossing the Allt na h-Eilde at 2km (1.5 miles). This is the natural outflow from Loch Eilde Mor though most of the water is diverted by pipeline to Blackwater Reservoir.

Our route follows the old drove road via Loch Chiarain, Glen Iolairean and Loch Treig to Fersit, but only as far as Loch Treig. The building of Treig Dam and Blackwater Reservoir dam, and the railways have all altered the route and barred its way north to Fersit.

Just below the dam the river meanders amongst some pleasant lochans.

MAP 28. BLACKWATER DAM

At 8km (5 miles) from Kinlochleven the north end of Blackwater Reservoir dam is reached. Here the outflow from Loch Eilde Mor is discharged into the reservoir. The dam (a long low concrete monstrosity) marks the end of the pleasant greenery of the River Leven and the start of the wild section of the route.

A couple of paths descend from a small cairn on the cross-country Loch Eilde Mor to Loch Chiarain path and our path

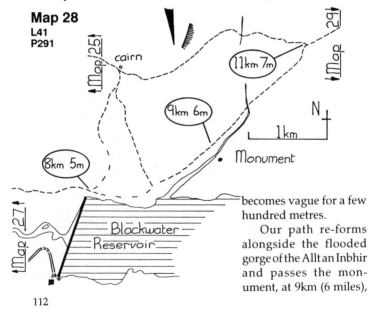

Map 28
L41
P291

becomes vague for a few hundred metres.

Our path re-forms alongside the flooded gorge of the Allt an Inbhir and passes the monument, at 9km (6 miles), to the First Vicar of St Albans who died here on 15 December 1887. This may prove the path (to Fersit?) was in regular use before the railway and the dams were built. Two years later the Bill was passed for the building of the West Highland line by Corrour and Loch Treig.

At 11km (7 miles) we are joined by the cross-country path from Loch Eilde Mor.

MAP 29. LOCH CHIARAIN

An old iron gate is passed just before the palatial two-storey bothy at Loch Chiarain 12.5km (8 miles) from Kinlochleven. A path opposite leads to the edge of Blackwater Reservoir. Was this linked to the dead-end path below Lubnachlach before the dam was built?

Our path follows the long glen north, now more remote than it used to be, with both Loch Chiarain bothy and Creaguianeach Lodge occupied.

Loch Treig is reached at last, some 19km (12 miles) from Kinlochleven. (This equates to reference point 30km / 19 miles from Fort William on map 6.) Here one can turn left for Staoineag, a

Loch Chiarain Bothy

further 3km (2 miles); or right for Loch Ossian Youth Hostel, a further 7km (4 miles).

The third option is to turn left, but only as far as Creaguaineach Lodge, then head north over the Lairig Leacach for Spean Bridge. Kinlochleven to Spean Bridge via Loch Chiarain, Gleann Iolairean and the eastern leg of the Lairig Leacach is 38km (24 miles).

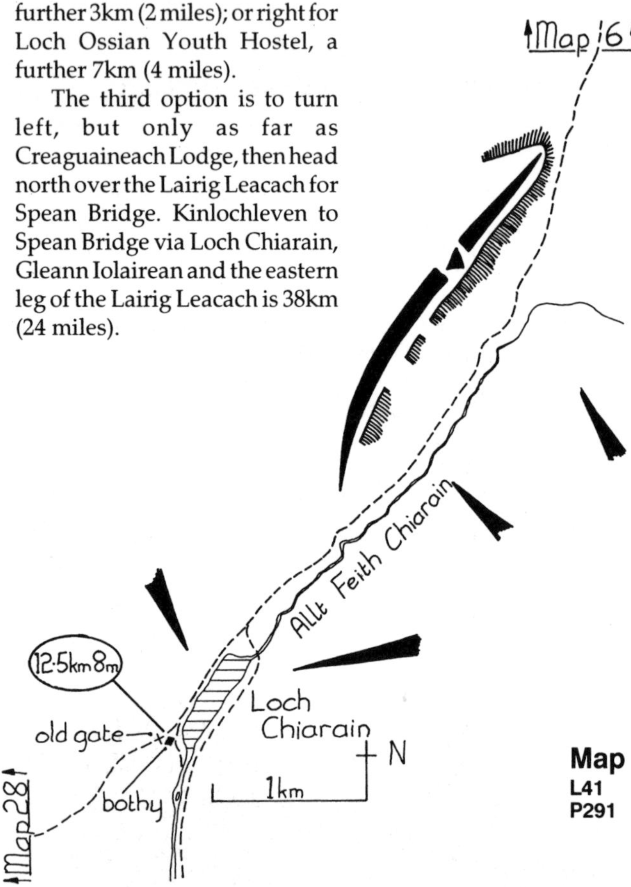

↑Map 6↑

Allt Feith Chiarain

12·5km 8m

old gate

↑Map 28↑

bothy

Loch Chiarain

N

1km

Map 29
L41
P291

WALK 4:
Drymen to Killin and Glen Almond

This walk is, by comparison with others in this book, a bit tame. Possibly comparable with the West Highland Way in that, at least as far as Killin, civilized overnight accommodation is available in

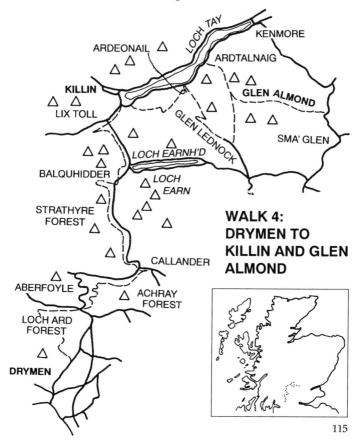

**WALK 4:
DRYMEN TO
KILLIN AND GLEN
ALMOND**

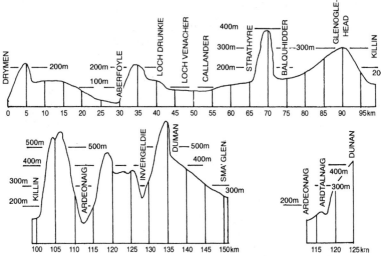

Gradient profile: Drymen to Killin and Glen Almond

pleasant villages placed at convenient distances along the route.

The start at Drymen allows for an equipment pick-up at Killin.

The walking is, however, pleasant giving an insight into a lost part of our infrastructure - our rural railway system that was. All with the prospect of a meal, a log fire and a comfortable bed at the end of each day.

Until Killin that is! Here the walk can be terminated or extended using a couple of wild camps. Gear can be posted on to Killin Post Office marked 'to be collected', extra food and fuel for your stove purchased before embarking on one of the two alternatives given from Killin to Sma' Glen - the finish.

The entire route - with the exception of Ben Chonzie - can be completed in the stalking season. Indeed this is recommended for the autumn colours, especially around Loch Drunkie.

The West Highland Way can be used from Milngavie to Drymen to lengthen the route and provide an alternative (more populous) starting point further south.

Interestingly almost the entire route can be cycled - the only diversion is to use the south Loch Tay road from Killin to Ardtalnaig.

116

Diagrammatical index to maps

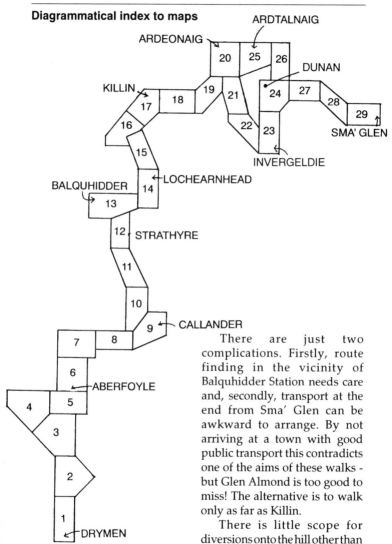

There are just two complications. Firstly, route finding in the vicinity of Balquhidder Station needs care and, secondly, transport at the end from Sma' Glen can be awkward to arrange. By not arriving at a town with good public transport this contradicts one of the aims of these walks - but Glen Almond is too good to miss! The alternative is to walk only as far as Killin.

There is little scope for diversions onto the hill other than Ben Chonzie, via Glen Lednock.

117

Walk 4: Drymen to Killin and Glen Almond - at a glance guide

Length:	98km (61 miles) to Killin 152km (94.5 miles) to Sma' Glen, reduced by 11km (7 miles) via Ardtalnaig. 4-7 days
Total climbing:	approximately 800m (to Killin) 1150m via Glen Lednock to Sma' Glen or 250m via Ardtalnaig to Sma' Glen
Accommodation:	B&B and youth hostels as far as Killin, then wild camping
Roads at:	Drymen (0km) Couligartan (near) 20km (12.5 miles) Milton 26.5km (16.5 miles) Aberfoyle 29km (18 miles) Callander (near) 49.54km (30.5 miles) Callander 53km (33 miles) Kilmahog 55.5km (34.5 miles) Pass of Leny 58km (36 miles) Strathyre 68km (42 miles) Balquhidder (near) 72.5km (45 miles) Balquhidder 75.5km (47 miles) Kingshouse 78.5km (48.5 miles) Lochearnhead 83km (51.5 miles) (1km off the route) Glenoglehead 89km (55 miles) Lix Toll 94km (58.5 miles) Killin 98km (61 miles) South Tayside 100km (62 miles) Ardeonaig 113km (70 miles) Invergeldie 127km (79 miles) or Ardtalnaig 118km (73 miles) Sma' Glen 152km (94.5 miles) (or via Ardtalnaig 141km (87.5 miles)
Bus services at:	Drymen 0km Aberfoyle 29km (18 miles) Callander 53km (33 miles) Strathyre 68km (42 miles) Lochearnhead 83km (51.5 miles) (1km off route) Killin 98km (61 miles) Sma' Glen 152km (94.5 miles) (Double check first!)
Rail services at:	Nil

Access to mountain groups en route:
> Ben Ledi (Pass of Leny)
> Ben Chonzie

O.S. maps (in their order of appearance):
> Landranger 57, 51, also 52 for Killin/Glen Almond
> Pathfinder 391 (only just!), 381, 369, 370, 358, 347,
> 334 and beyond Killin: 335, 348, 336

MAP 1. DRYMEN

Drymen, once a staging post on the cattle drove route from Knapdale and Kintyre to Falkirk Tryst, is the starting point for our fourth Walk. It is a pleasant village with shops, tourist information and a variety of pubs and B&B accommodation.

The walk heads north up the Drymen Road, a metalled public road, but thankfully quiet as it leads up into Loch Ard Forest.

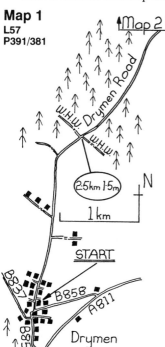

Map 1
L57
P391/381

After 2.5km (1.5 miles) the route is crossed by the West Highland Way. It is obvious, therefore, that the West Highland Way may be used as an alternative start to this walk, diverting at Drymen to explore The Trossachs rather than heading north by Loch Lomond for Bridge of Orchy and Rannoch Moor.

Our route continues up Drymen Road.

MAP 2. DRYMEN ROAD

As the public road descends to Dalmary and Gartmore, and about 250m before Drymen Road Cottage, we arrive at a car park at 6.5km (4 miles). Here a road arrives from our right, from the A81 via Hoish, and we turn left along the continuation of this metalled forest road, ignoring the further left turn onto the high-level forest tracks and continuing over the steel bridge. Here we can see the Loch Katrine aqueduct, an interesting feat of engineering which we follow to the great aqueduct above Couligartan.

We continue past Corrie, that is the Corrie at GR 490946, and not shown on the O.S. Landranger map (not the one at GR 493953 which is shown on the O.S. Landranger map!).

Passing over Manhole Bridge and ignoring left and right turns we head due north. At 10km (6 miles) we again continue north, thankful that at last the metalled surface gives way to the crunch of gravel under foot.

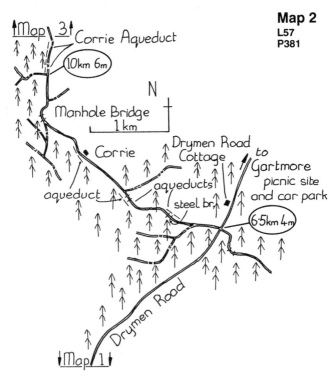

Map 2
L57
P381

MAP 3. CLASHMORE

The complexities of the Loch Ard Forest tracks need careful navigation and a compass can be used to confirm which track is which.

We by-pass firstly a gated track on our right then another track on the left before a steep zigzag takes us up over a crest which then descends to a crossroads. Here we take the gated track on the right which descends alongside Gartlachtach Burn to Clashmore.

Immediately after Clashmore we are joined by a track from the right and then keep left at the fork a few metres further on. A left turn after about 300m brings us to a wide crossroads at 13km (8.5 miles), from which we go straight on, or just north of due west.

(A right turn at the above crossroads provides a short-cut to Kirkton and Aberfoyle should the weather conditions dictate - no-one will know you cheated!)

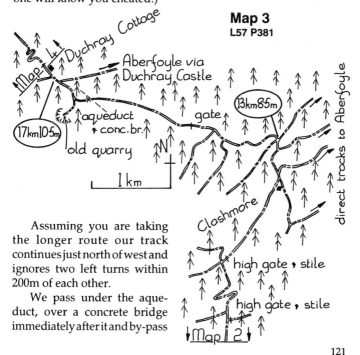

Map 3
L57 P381

Assuming you are taking the longer route our track continues just north of west and ignores two left turns within 200m of each other.

We pass under the aqueduct, over a concrete bridge immediately after it and by-pass a rough track to an old quarry where rock was extracted for the aqueduct.

Ignoring right and left turns we pass Duchray Cottage at 17km (10.5 miles) and cross the gated Duchray Bridge. The Duchray Water, when joined by the outflow from Loch Ard, becomes the River Forth.

MAP 4. LOCH ARD

From Duchray Bridge at 17km (11 miles) we climb steeply up several hairpin bends. We walk past one huge aqueduct and pass under the second to emerge at a crossroads, the left-hand track also having passed under the aqueduct.

From this crossroads we walk straight ahead, heading north-west. We arrive at the complex junction at Couligartan, at 20km (12.5 miles), where two right turns take us on our easterly route to Aberfoyle whilst a right and a left takes us to Loch Ard Youth Hostel by Kinlochard. (The hostel is 4km/2.5 miles off our route.)

Heading east along the south shore of Loch Ard the peninsular loop track overlooking Eilean Gorm and an ancient crannog can be

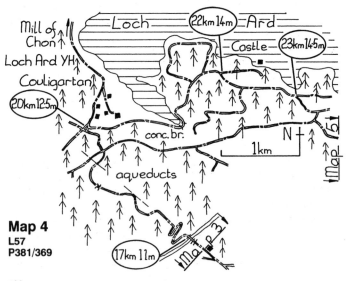

Map 4
L57
P381/369

Aqueduct

ignored. We arrive at a junction at 22km (14 miles) at which point a rough track runs down to the ruins of the Duke of Murdoch's castle which is something of a disappointment as it is on an island and there is not much of it left.

Proceeding south-east, then east, past a right turn to a dead end we arrive at a junction at 23km (14.5 miles) at which point we bear right (south-east, then in 400m turn sharp right (south-west), then after 150m turn left (south-east). This bit of careful navigating brings us alongside Lochan a'Ghleannain, where it will be difficult to resist the temptation to rest awhile.

MAP 5. ABERFOYLE

After leaving the delights of Lochan a'Ghleannain and by-passing the track passing around its south shore at 25km (15.5 miles), head east to a 'T' junction, then left to emerge on the public road at Milton at 26.5km (16.5 miles).

The minor road is followed for 2km (1.5 miles) to the village of Aberfoyle at 29km (18 miles), with its range of shops, pubs and B&B accommodation. Aberfoyle is a pleasant enough spot to spend a rest day, perhaps including a visit to David Marshall Lodge, a Forest

Map 5
L57 P369

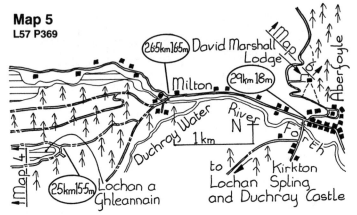

Enterprise visitor centre just above the village.

Although 29km is a fairly long first day, the route can be shortened from Clashmore although this omits the interest of the aqueducts. Better perhaps to stay at Loch Ard Youth Hostel, leaving a half-day walk into Aberfoyle, and time for David Marshall Lodge.

MAP 6. ACHRAY FOREST

Leave Aberfoyle at 29km (18 miles) by the tortuous Duke's Pass road up to David Marshall Lodge. A complex web of forest walks surround the Lodge but the aim is to locate the footbridge 300m due east of the lodge, at 'x', from which it is a simple matter to gain the forest track 100m to the north of the bridge.

Having reached the track turn left, west, round the big right-hand bend, turn left, and continue to gain the crossroads at 31km (19.5 miles). Go straight ahead at the crossroads and sharp left after 300m.

We emerge at a crossroads at 33.5km (21 miles) and go straight on. At the next junction turn sharp right (east) then take the right-hand gated branch at the fork (south-east). A further left turn and we emerge, through a further gate, by the southern arm of the beautiful Loch Drunkie at the junction at 36km (22.5 miles).

Here we turn right to follow the lochside. The autumn colours around Loch Drunkie are stunning.

34km 21·5m

car pk

gates

gates

Map 7

Loch Drunkie

33·5km 21m

36km 22·5m

N

1 km

pole gte.

to Meall Ear

333 m

31km 19·5m

Duke's Pass

Map 6
L57
P369

D.M. Lodge

x

Map 5

29km 18m Aberfoyle

MAP 7. LOCH DRUNKIE

At 38.5km (24 miles) we arrive at a car park, toilets and picnic area. This can be a very busy area on fine summer weekends. Our route follows the shore of Loch Drunkie, by-passing the track at 40km (25 miles), which returns to the car park, by-passing a further left turn just after a gate, 250m ahead and straight ahead at the oblique crossroads.

We arrive at the junction at 41km (25.5 miles) where a sharp right turn takes us away from the Forest Drive. A signpost by the gate explains the Loch Venachar Cycleway - which is also a footpath. This is a purpose-built section of path built as part of a cycleway from Glasgow to Killin - at the time of writing still in the process of being developed.

The new path is well engineered yet unobtrusive as it winds its way along the wooded lochside.

Map 7 L57 P369

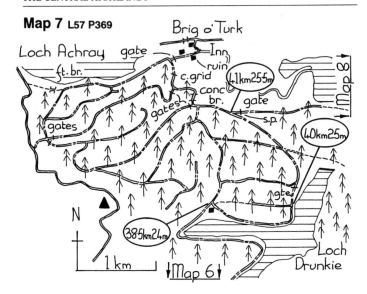

MAP 8. LOCH VENACHAR

After a short break on the thoughtfully provided seats the lochside path continues, only to end all too soon just after the footbridge at 44km (27.5 miles).

Here the private road to Invertrossachs is joined and we continue east towards Callander. One consequence of the designated cycleway may be observed in the number of 'strictly private' signs south of the

Map 8
L57
P369

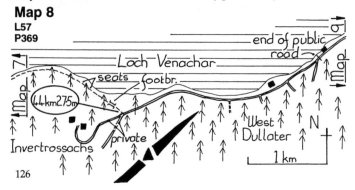

private road. One wonders whether these restrictions have arisen as a result of the cycleway, in order to keep the increased number of walkers and cyclists on the designated route.

The end of the public road is reached at a gate at East Lodge.

MAP 9. CALLANDER

The public road is followed towards Callander via the junction at 49.5km (30.5 miles). Here it is possible to by-pass Callander by crossing the Eas Gobhain by Gartchonzie Bridge and following a new footpath alongside the A821 to the old railway before Kilmahog. This shortens the route by 4.5km (3 miles) but by-passes the delights (and accommodation) of Callander.

The public road is easily followed into Callander at 53km (33 miles), a convenient 24km (15 miles) from Aberfoyle. Indeed, a feature of this walk is the strategic location of pleasant villages with accommodation and all facilities and comforts - at least until Killin, after which you are on your own!

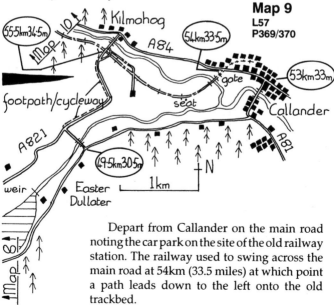

Depart from Callander on the main road noting the car park on the site of the old railway station. The railway used to swing across the main road at 54km (33.5 miles) at which point a path leads down to the left onto the old trackbed.

We follow the obvious line of the railway, well used by the locals and provided with seats, until the road crossing at 55.5km (34.5 miles) where a new road bridge over the railway trackbed has replaced the old. Here the 'short-cut' from Gartchonzie Bridge joins us as we head north-west into the Pass of Leny.

MAP 10. PASS OF LENY

The A84 - an old military road built in the years 1748 to 1753 by General Caulfield - follows the route of the old railway from Callander to Killin Junction station as the geography squeezes the available routes together here, at the Pass of Leny, as at Glenoglehead.

At the Falls of Leny, at 57km (35.5 miles), the railway line used to cross the river, soon to cross back again. Both bridges are long gone but a new path has been built around this obstacle, rejoining the railway trackbed at 58km (36 miles). This section of path is another purpose-built part of the cycle/walking route from Glasgow to Killin.

The next short section of trackbed serves as a car park with access over the Garbh Uisge river by road bridge from the A84. The track forking left is by-passed as we stay on the old trackbed along the west shore of Loch Lubnaig.

Map 10
L57
P369/358

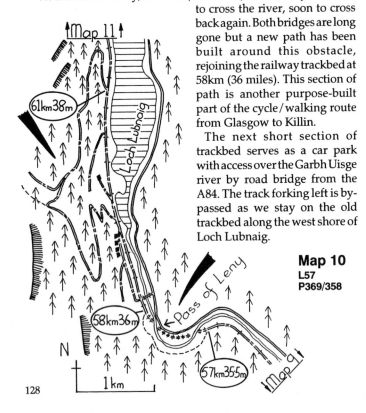

128   1 km

The head of Loch Treig (Walk 3)
Gateway to the wilderness - Strathossian House (Walk 3)

Loch Drunkie (Walk 4)
Ardtalnaig Glen (Walk 4)

Forestry tracks on the left can be ignored as we proceed, past the forest cabins and north past the junctions at 61km (38 miles).

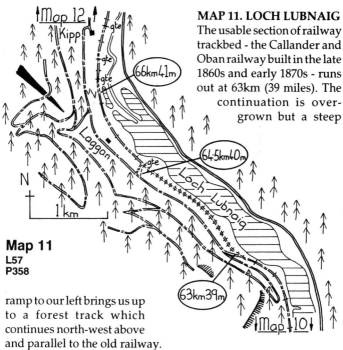

MAP 11. LOCH LUBNAIG

The usable section of railway trackbed - the Callander and Oban railway built in the late 1860s and early 1870s - runs out at 63km (39 miles). The continuation is overgrown but a steep

Map 11
L57
P358

ramp to our left brings us up to a forest track which continues north-west above and parallel to the old railway.

At 64.5km (40 miles) the way ahead is barred by a large ford but all is not lost for a footpath cuts down to the right to regain the old railway trackbed by a gate which bars access to the right, so we turn left to continue north-west.

After the zigzag path at 66km (41 miles) joins us on the left a succession of gates leads us north to the site of the old Strathyre Station.

MAP 12. STRATHYRE

A new footbridge crosses the River Balvag, leading us into Strathyre at 68km (42 miles).

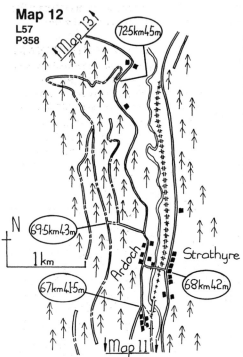

Map 12
L57
P358

72.5km 45m

Map 13

69.5km 43m

N

1km

67km 41.5m

Ardoch

Strathyre

68km 42m

Map 11

Although only 14.5km (9 miles) from Callander, Strathyre is a useful overnight stopping point - especially if no accommodation has been pre-booked in Balquhidder.

On leaving Strathyre I suggest the inclusion of a hill loop of forest track, firstly to enjoy the views and secondly to avoid some (quiet) road walking.

After re-crossing the old railway and river in Strathyre turn right in Ardoch and then left on a metalled forest road to the higher 'T' junction at 69.5km (43 miles).

The track continues to climb and is joined by a track from the left just before its summit and a chain 'gate'. After admiring the view from the big bend the track descends steeply to 72.5km (45 miles), the last 100m or so involving diving through broom bushes which have grown over the track! Turn left on the road to Balquhidder.

MAP 13. BALQUHIDDER
Some road walking now as we follow the minor road around the Balquhidder loop.

The village, at 75.5km (47 miles) has forest walks around the site of Rob Roy's grave.

There are three alternative ways between Balquhidder and Glen

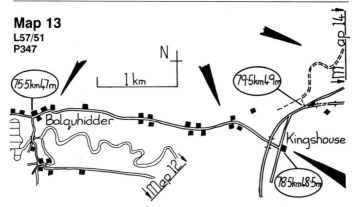

Map 13
L57/51
P347

N

1 km

75·5km47m

79·5km49m

Balquhidder

Kingshouse

Map 12

78·5km48·5m

Dochart. The first is directly above Balquhidder, via Kirkton Glen to Ledcharrie, but the connection to Killin Junction is across open farmland, the right of way ending at Ledcharrie.

The second route is via Glen Dubh and Glen Kendrum - a track runs over the bealach at GR 542248 although this is not shown on the O.S. maps at the time of writing. This is not a right of way and shares its complex start with the third and my recommended route - shown on the map as the Glen Ogle Trail.

We head, therefore, to Kingshouse at 78.5km (48.5 miles). Here the new road has taken the place of the old railway line. At Kingshouse the villagers campaigned for their own railway station and ended up building it themselves.

We are obliged to follow the main road to reference point 79.5km (49 miles). At this point a path heads north-west for 100m through a wood. The exact position of the start of this path is identifiable by the signpost 'Balquhidder Station' which indeed used to lie at the opposite side of the main road.

After the 100m length of path, go through a gate in the wall and turn right. The path follows the tortuous route of the old military road, over wet ground and several small fords. The trick is to follow the line of the original road - it is not now a track as such!

MAP 14. LOCHEARNHEAD
The old military road eventually improves to a proper track and

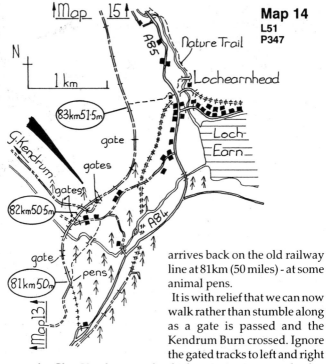

arrives back on the old railway line at 81km (50 miles) - at some animal pens.

It is with relief that we can now walk rather than stumble along as a gate is passed and the Kendrum Burn crossed. Ignore the gated tracks to left and right but note the Glen Kendrum track which arrives via an overbridge and gated ramp on our right, this being at 82km (50.5 miles).

A further gate lies across the railway and another after about 1km (half a mile) - all is now thankfully plain sailing again after the complexities of the last few kilometres.

At 83km (51.5 miles) a steep path leads directly down to Lochearnhead. This may be used if an overnight has been arranged here. Note from here the low-level railway passing along the north shore of Loch Earn - another cycleway perhaps?

From Lochearnhead, or at least from reference point 83km (51.5 miles), we continue north.

MAP 15. GLEN OGLE

At 86km (53.5 miles) we pass over a substantial viaduct - care! bits of the walls are missing. Looking up the glen from here the A85, old A85, military road and railway can be traced as the narrow glen brings all these together at Glenoglehead.

Beyond the viaduct a rough section is encountered, a flooding cutting and landslip. If too wet this can be avoided by footpath and road to the right, rejoining the railway at Glenoglehead.

The rough section ends at 88km (54.5 miles) at which point we are joined by a forest track which runs on the old trackbed to Glenoglehead Station at 89km (55 miles).

The Callander and Oban Railway was opened from Callander to the old Killin Station in 1870, the Killin to Tyndrum section being opened in 1873. It was not until 1886 that the Killin Branch was opened, including the building of Killin Junction interchange station and renaming the old Killin Station Glenoglehead.

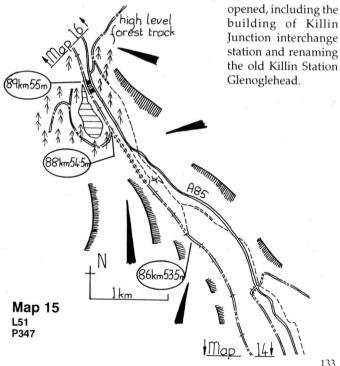

Map 15
L51
P347

Map 16
L51
P347/334

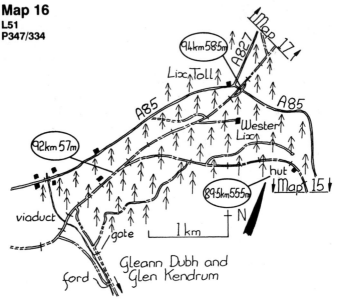

MAP 16. LIX TOLL

From Glenoglehead we stay on the old railway passing an old platelayers' hut at 89.5km (55.5 miles) which provides shelter if needed (though no comforts!).

We proceed to the site of Killin Junction station at 92km (57 miles). Once a scene of activity with three platforms, a siding and two signal boxes, only the platform and ruined cottages remain. A little further on towards Tyndrum the Ardchyle Viaduct at the outflow of Gleann Dubh stands as a monument to the railway builders.

However, we double back, on the descending line of the Killin Branch, heading for Lix Toll at 94km (58.5 miles) where the bridge has been demolished and a track loops down to the road which now has to be crossed. The railway is gated at both sides and the old branchline rejoined as we head for Killin.

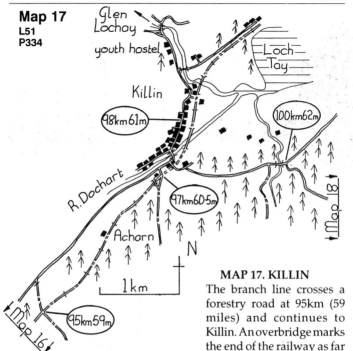

Map 17
L51
P334

Glen Lochay

youth hostel

Loch Tay

Killin

98km 61m

100km 62m

R. Dochart

97km 60·5m

Map 18

Acharn

N

1 km

Map 16

95km 59m

MAP 17. KILLIN

The branch line crosses a forestry road at 95km (59 miles) and continues to Killin. An overbridge marks the end of the railway as far as we are concerned and a forest road joins from the right. Here we turn left and emerge on the main road just above the Falls of Dochart at 97km (60.5 miles).

A right turn takes us over the Bridge of Dochart and into Killin at 98km (61 miles), yet another pleasant village complete with accommodation, hotels, B&Bs and a Youth Hostel.

It is worth tracing the old railway to the old Killin Station and the Loch Tay Station where the little branchline train used to connect with the Loch Tay steamers.

At Killin a decision has to be made - or preferably at the planning stage of the walk for from here the nature of the walk changes. Ahead lies wild country: Ben Chonzie, Glen Lednock, Glen Almond and a finish at Sma' Glen. Check bus services - or arrange a lift - carefully!

Killin

My suggestion would be to post camping gear (not fuel!) on to Killin 'to be collected', stock up food and fuel in the shops in Killin and continue the walk prepared to camp wild.

Alternatively the walk may be concluded at Killin but that would be to miss the chance to scale the isolated (from other Munros) Ben Chonzie and explore the beautiful Glen Almond!

Leave Killin (if you are still with me!) by the minor south Loch Tay road to reference point 100km (62 miles), just past the Achmore Burn bridge. Turn right through a gate up the metalled Lochan Breaclaich reservoir road - a steady plod up to nearly 600m awaits!

MAP 18. LOCHAN BREACLAICH

At 102km (63.5 miles) a mast is passed. Usually a mast signifies the top of a hill must be near - not here! We continue below the Lochan Breaclaich dam and taking care not to turn left into the quarry at 104km (64.5 miles) the track continues around the far (north) side of the lochan. A left turn strikes up the hillside for the final section to the summit, the metalled road having been left behind at the dam.

Lochan Breaclaich is used to provide additional catchment for

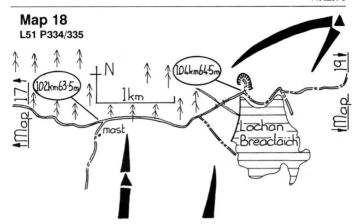

Map 18
L51 P334/335

Loch Lednock - via tunnels and the pipeline encountered on the descent from the top mast.

MAP 19. CEANN CREAGACH

The track makes its tortuous way past the summit mast and drops, at first steeply, to the pipeline.

At 109km (67.5 miles), and about 50m before our track takes a sharp turn right to follow the pipeline, a vague path turns left. This is followed but may be lost as it is indistinct. The aim is to head for the gate at the north-west corner of the rectangular wood at 110km (68 miles).

A rough track materialises just before this gate and becomes an improved Landrover track 600m further on after two further gates and a ford.

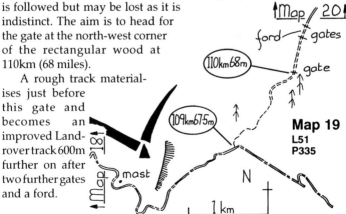

Map 19
L51
P335

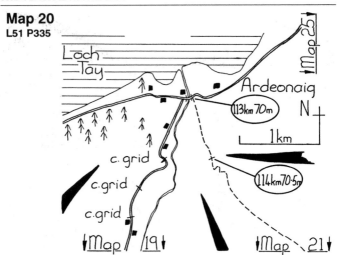

Map 20
L51 P335

Loch Tay
Ardeonaig
113km 70m
N
1km
c. grid
c.grid
c.grid
114km 70·5m
Map 19
Map 21
Map 25

MAP 20. ARDEONAIG

Past Braentrian the farm road is metalled with cattle grids as we descend to Ardeonaig at 113km (70 miles) on the shore of Loch Tay. Ardeonaig was one of the ports of call for the Loch Tay steamboats which used to ply these waters.

The route from Ardeonaig to Glen Lednock was part of the drovers' route from Skye, via south Loch Tay to the Tryst, or fair, at Comrie. Indeed plans were afoot for this well-developed drove road to be improved by Telford. However, as Falkirk Tryst became more important than Comrie the main drovers' route became Glen Ogle, Callander and Doune - the route of the present-day main road; and, indeed, the Callander and Oban Railway.

Continue onto map 25, p143, for the shorter route to Glen Almond via Ardtalnaig but omitting Glen Lednock and Ben Chonzie.

The route from Ardeonaig runs almost due south. The start is vague, climbing enclosed fields, but the aim is to head for a stile at 114km (70.5 miles) from which point the right of way becomes better defined as a path.

MAP 21. LOCH LEDNOCK

The watershed is crossed at 117km (72.5 miles) after climbing out of

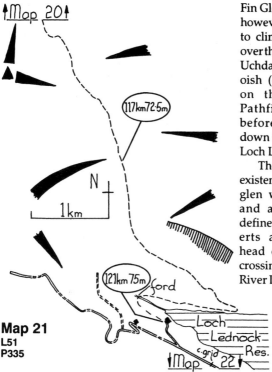

Fin Glen. The path, however, continues to climb for 500m over the shoulder of Uchdan Mhic Thaoish (only named on the 1:25,000 Pathfinder map) before dropping down to the side of Loch Lednock.

The path was in existence before the glen was flooded and a less well-defined path diverts around the head of the loch, crossing the infant River Lednock by a

ford to emerge at an unattractive power station at 121km (75 miles).

We take the metalled road, rising from the power station to head south-east some distance above the shore of the reservoir.

MAP 22. LEDNOCK DAM

The metalled road arrives at reference point 123km (76.5 miles). Here a zigzag road climbs to the watershed on our right but, to take a shorter route on a footpath we turn left and, from the next bend in the road below us, take the remnant of the old path as it re-emerges from the depths of the loch.

This path rejoins the metalled reservoir road at 125km (77.5 miles). We proceed down the glen, over a planked bridge and over

139

Lednock Dam

a couple of filled-in cattle grids to join the road to the dam at 126km (78 miles).

Continue south-east down the glen.

Map 22
L51
P348

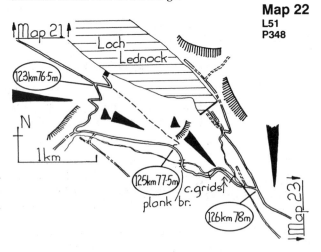

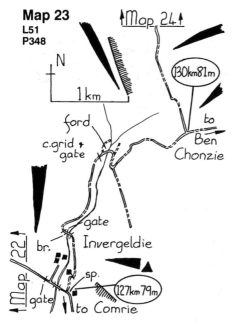

Map 23
L51
P348

N

1 km

ford

c.grid
gate

ford

Map 24

130km 81m

to
Ben
Chonzie

gate

br.   Invergeldie

Map 22

sp.

gate   to Comrie

127km 79m

MAP 23. INVERGELDIE

A gate brings us out onto the public road by Invergeldie and some 300m further on, at a bend in the road by the old schoolhouse at 129km (79 miles), a Scottish Rights of Way Society signpost 'Ardtalnaig' directs us up by the Invergeldie burn and Ben Chonzie.

At Coishavachan a sharp right before the farm buildings, then left, brings us to a bridge over the burn after which a gate leads us onto the open hillside. The track is followed, via a further gate, ford and zigzag up from this crossing of the burn to reference point 130km (81 miles).

From here Ben Chonzie is within easy striking distance - head east up the steepening track to a sharp right-hand bend at GR 769293 then north-east to gain the crest of the broad ridge to its summit. Our route is rejoined by heading north-west from the summit to the watershed at reference point 134km (83 miles) on map 24.

Our walking route, by-passing Ben Chonzie, continues north from reference point 130km (81 miles).

MAP 24. DUNAN

The track deteriorates into a rough path as it reaches the watershed at 134km (83 miles). From here a path descends to the footbridge 300m below Dunan at 136km (84.5 miles). Dunan is a roofed ruin providing shelter but not in a fit state to be used as a bothy.

The end of the track in Glen Almond

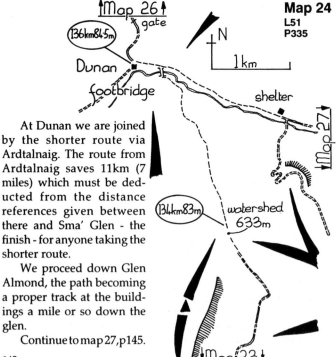

Map 24
L51
P335

Map 26
gate

136km84·5m

Dunan

footbridge

shelter

Map 27

134km83m   watershed
633m

Map 23

At Dunan we are joined by the shorter route via Ardtalnaig. The route from Ardtalnaig saves 11km (7 miles) which must be deducted from the distance references given between there and Sma' Glen - the finish - for anyone taking the shorter route.

We proceed down Glen Almond, the path becoming a proper track at the buildings a mile or so down the glen.

Continue to map 27, p145.

142

Map 25

L51
P335

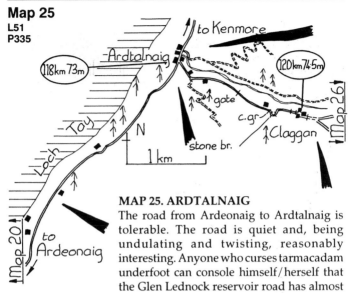

MAP 25. ARDTALNAIG

The road from Ardeonaig to Ardtalnaig is tolerable. The road is quiet and, being undulating and twisting, reasonably interesting. Anyone who curses tarmacadam underfoot can console himself/herself that the Glen Lednock reservoir road has almost as much metalled surface.

At last Ardtalnaig is reached at 118km (73 miles) and a right turn is taken before the bridge to climb up the metalled farm road to Claggan.

At Claggan, at 120km (74.5 miles), go straight ahead through two gates into the farmyard, between the buildings. Turn right after the second gate then immediately left, then straight ahead through another two gates. The track then forks; take the left branch. This route is intrusive but it is a right of way.

MAP 26. GLEANN A CHILLEINE

The track crosses the bridge before the ruin at Tullichglass which is reached by a couple of rough tracks from the main route at 121km (75 miles).

The track heads south up this straight glen, the scene suddenly becoming wild after Claggan and Tullichglass.

Oddly Gleann a Chilleine and Glen Almond were used neither as drovers' route nor for military purposes. The drovers' route takes

143

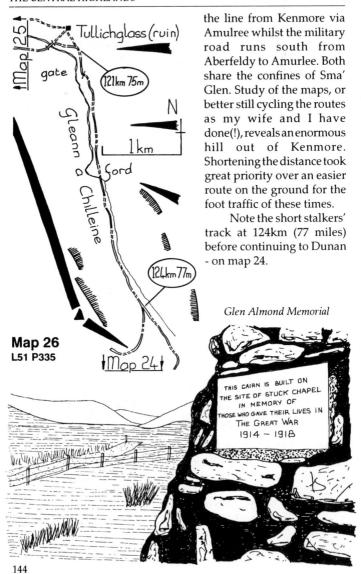

Map 26
L51 P335

Tullichglass (ruin)

gate

121km 75m

N

1 km

Gleann a Chilleine

ford

124km 77m

Map 25

Map 24

the line from Kenmore via Amulree whilst the military road runs south from Aberfeldy to Amurlee. Both share the confines of Sma' Glen. Study of the maps, or better still cycling the routes as my wife and I have done(!), reveals an enormous hill out of Kenmore. Shortening the distance took great priority over an easier route on the ground for the foot traffic of these times.

Note the short stalkers' track at 124km (77 miles) before continuing to Dunan - on map 24.

Glen Almond Memorial

THIS CAIRN IS BUILT ON
THE SITE OF STUCK CHAPEL
IN MEMORY OF
THOSE WHO GAVE THEIR LIVES IN
THE GREAT WAR
1914 – 1918

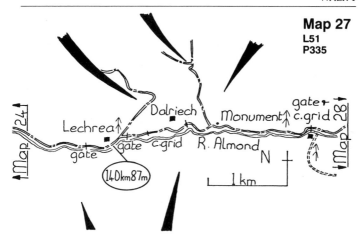

Map 27
L51
P335

MAP 27. UPPER GLEN ALMOND

Glen Almond is a gem. A long straight glen with a feeling of both space and, in its upper reaches, solitude.

The ruins at Lechrea at 140km (87 miles) were in a state of

Lechrea, Glen Almond

collapse on my last visit so don't rely on the roof for shelter!

Just before the monument the Stuck Chapel Burn is crossed. Note the Stuck Chapel Spout waterfall and Stuck Chapel Craig above. The monument, built on the site of Stuck Chapel, is in memory of those who lost their lives in the First World War. The outer wall of the old chapel can still be traced on the ground. It may now seem an odd place for a chapel but Glen Almond would have been well populated in times gone by. Many now remote glens used to have their own school.

With these thoughts we plod on to Sma' Glen.

MAP 28. AUCHNAFREE

Before Auchnafree is reached note the memorial to John Pollock - a recent tribute to a local shepherd. These memorials give not only a sense of history to Glen Almond but give a slightly sad sense of the glen seeing happier times in more populous days.

The grand lodge of Auchnafree is passed, two tracks leading up to this fine building. The second, main, driveway leaves our track at reference point 145km (90 miles).

We pass the farm at Conichan, below the precipitous Eagle's Rock.

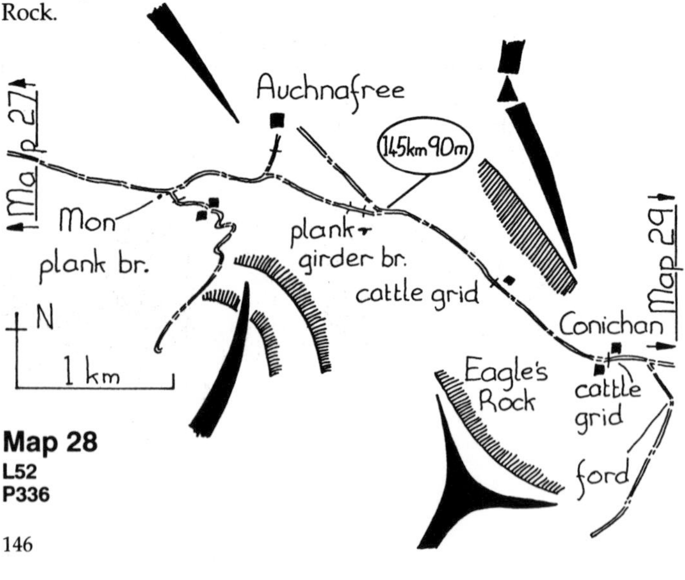

Map 28
L52
P336

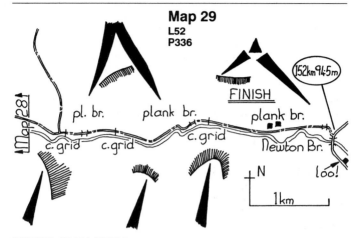

Map 29
L52
P336

MAP 29. SMA' GLEN

The track, possibly by now seeming endless, continues down the glen to reach the main road by Newton Bridge, at 152m (94.5 miles), at the head of Sma' Glen - effectively a continuation of Glen Almond. Here we meet the drovers' and military road routes coming over the hill from Amulree just to the north.

Here it is hoped that your transport arrangements work out. Only careful planning will ensure the walk ends with a bus or a lift available - the alternative is a long slog into Crieff. One consolation - if you have a long wait at the Newton Bridge car park, there is a loo!

WALK: 5
Dunkeld to Aboyne

A long and hilly cross-country walk of 142km (88 miles) starting from Dunkeld and Birnam railway station. The route passes through Kirkmichael before heading cross-country to Loch Muick and Ballater, crossing the mountains twice more to Glen Doll and back to Deeside.

A slightly shorter route (map 15) uses the Mounth Road from Glen Doll to Glen Muick.

I again suggest a general south-west to north-easterly direction

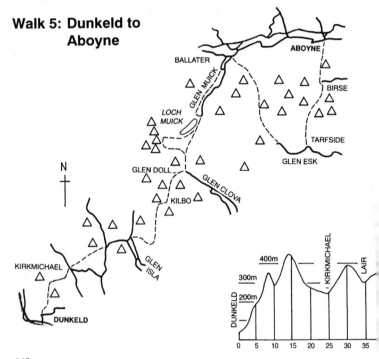

Walk 5: Dunkeld to Aboyne

as it is more comfortable to walk with both prevailing wind and afternoon sun behind. On the subject of weather it is worth noting that rainfall in this region is about half that encountered on the west coast. Midges, too, tend to be less troublesome in the east.

Accommodation can, with careful pre-planning, be arranged using B&Bs and Glen Doll Youth Hostel. This may lead to some long days which should be feasible without a tent, sleeping bag, stove and a mountain of food!

There are small sections of both pathless terrain - requiring care in navigating - and road walking.

The walk can be ended at Ballater (92.5km/57 miles) and the remainder completed as a circuit from Aboyne, taking in the picturesque route up the full length of Glen Tanar.

Public roads are encountered at intervals sometimes giving long(ish) days out.

Inclusion of adjacent mountains may dictate a different approach of shorter days with full wild camping kit.

**Gradient profile:
Dunkeld to Aboyne**

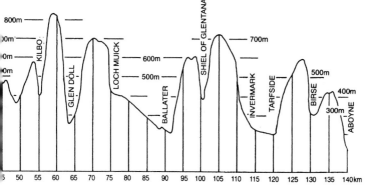

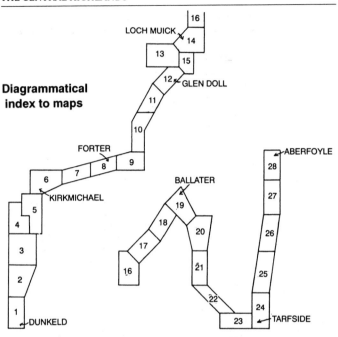

**Diagrammatical
index to maps**

Walk 5: Dunkeld to Aboyne - at a glance guide

Length:	142km (88 miles) - the Mounth Road reduces this by 5km (3 miles) maps 12-14. 5-8 days
Total climbing:	approximately 3200m (I said it was hilly!)
Accommodation:	B&Bs and Youth Hostel (campsite at Glen Doll)
Roads at:	Dunkeld 0-2km (0-1 miles) Kirkmichael 29km (18 miles) Lair 35km (22 miles) to: Glen Doll 62.5km (39 miles) Spittal of Glenmuick 78km (48 miles) Mill of Sterin 88km (54.5 miles) to: Ballater 92.5km (57 miles) to: Bridge of Muick 93.5km (58 miles) Invermark 113km (70 miles) to:

Tarfside 120km (74.5 miles)
Ballochan 131km (81 miles) (road 1km/0.5 mile away)
Aboyne 142km (88 miles)

Bus services at: Dunkeld 0km
Kirkmichael 29km (18 miles)
Glen Doll 62.5km (39 miles)
Ballater 92.5km (57 miles)
Aboyne 142km (88 miles)

Rail services at: Dunkeld and Birnam 0km

Access to mountain groups en route:
Mayar and Driesh
Broad Cairn - Lochnagar
Mount Keen

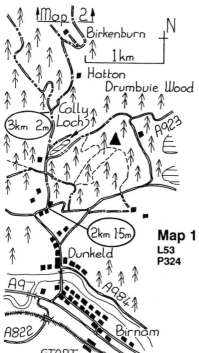

O.S. maps (in their order of appearance):
Landranger 53, 43, 44
Pathfinder 324, 310, 295*, 296, 283, 270, 256, 257, 271, 284
*Map 295 is especially useful

MAP 1. DUNKELD

Setting off from Dunkeld and Birnam railway station the route immediately heads north up the main street in Dunkeld - complete with tea shops and numerous distractions! It is, however, a full day's walk to Kirkmichael (the probable first stop) so resist temptation and continue north, rising above the town to reference point 2km (1.5 miles).

Dunkeld, as well as being a route centre of both

Map 1
L53
P324

151

drovers' and military roads, was once the terminus of the Perth and Dunkeld Railway Company. This situation existed from 1856 to 1863 when the little branch line (which never paid its way) became part of the Perth to Inverness main line.

A signpost points north indicating 'Public footpath to Kirkmichael 15' and 'The Glack'. No further signposts indicate our route, so take care to follow these directions!

Ignore both left and right turnings until reference point 3km (2 miles). Here a right fork keeps us on the main track which follows the zigzags around Birkenburn.

MAP 2. MILL DAM

The main track is followed, by-passing The Glack on our right until a rough track branches right at the outflow of Mill Dam at 6km (4 miles).

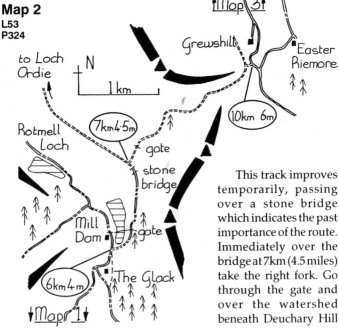

Map 2
L53
P324

to Loch Ordie

N

1 km

↑Map 3↑

Grewshill

Easter Riemore

10km 6m

Rotmell Loch

7km 4.5m

gate

stone bridge

Mill Dam

gate

6km 4m

The Glack

↓Map 1↓

This track improves temporarily, passing over a stone bridge which indicates the past importance of the route. Immediately over the bridge at 7km (4.5 miles) take the right fork. Go through the gate and over the watershed beneath Deuchary Hill to reach a metalled road just below Grewshill at 10km (6 miles) - a twin-trunked tree marks the junction.

We turn left (north) on the metalled road which links Riemore Lodge to the public road at Butterstone.

MAP 3. LOCH ORDIE

At reference point 11km (7 miles) the metalled road swings right to the Lodge and we carry straight on towards Loch Ordie, a fishing loch with its lodge surrounded by rhododendrons at its south-west corner.

After the gate and stile we arrive at a crossroads of old tracks and turn right to head east then north alongside the Buckney Burn. This track is severely overgrown and in need of use or it will be lost forever.

Ignore the right turn at 14km (9 miles) and continue north. The track now becomes a path in one of the old ruts formed when vehicles used the track.

Lochordie Lodge

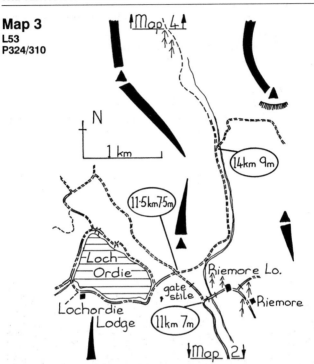

Map 3
L53
P324/310

MAP 4. LOCHAN OISINNEACH

Note the link track (not on the OS map) joining us on the left some 500m before another stone bridge at 16km (10 miles). The rough track before the tin hut does not provide a way into Strathardle - I know, I've tried it!

Eventually Lochan Oisinneach Beag is reached (the word Beag - small - is omitted on the Landranger map). North of the loch the track bends left to head just north of due west, at reference point 19km (12 miles). End of track!

From here we leave the track and head NNE keeping a low crag on the left and heading for the watershed just beyond a clump of trees. From the watershed head due north to reach Loch Eisg Burn at GR 041571 and follow it to GR 044575, reference point 20.5km (13 miles). Here the burn turns left (north-west) but we continue in a north-easterly direction - use your compass!

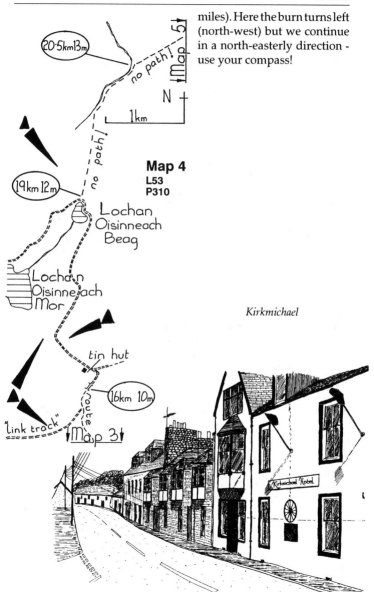

20·5km 13m

no path!

Map 5

N

1km

Map 4
L53
P310

no path!

19km 12m

Lochan Oisinneach Beag

Lochan Oisinneach Mor

Kirkmichael

tin hut

16km 10m

route

"link track"

Map 3

Kirkmichael Hotel

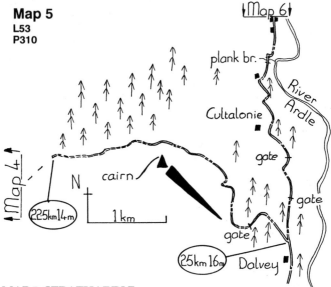

MAP 5. STRATHARDLE

After a mile of featureless level walking we arrive at GR 057583 at the end of the rough track that leads us to Kirkmichael. Ahead lies a new plantation and a low crag falls away to our right 200m before we reach the track. Follow this track to the east, keeping the new plantation on the left.

The track swings south-east and descends, entering the woods at a gate. The main track is reached at 25km (16 miles). Turn left. It is a simple matter to follow the main track from here into the centre of the picturesque village of Kirkmichael at 29km (18 miles).

MAP 6. KIRKMICHAEL

The section from Kirkmichael to Lair appears from the O.S. map to go right through the grounds of Ashintully Castle. Don't believe it! The route is complex but is waymarked. It is a good idea to have the O.S. Pathfinder map (no. 295) handy - the route isn't shown, but at least the walls and fences are.

From the bridge in Kirkmichael, cross the River Ardle opposite

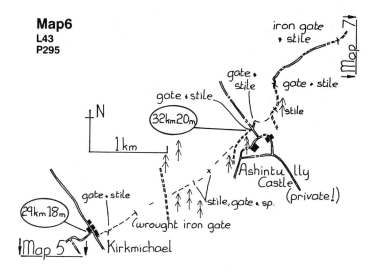

Map6
L43
P295

iron gate
• stile

gate •
stile

gate • stile

gate • stile

stile

N

32km20m

1km

Ashintully
Castle
(private!)

gate • stile

29km18m

stile, gate • sp.

(wrought iron gate

Map 5

Kirkmichael

the Kirkmichael Hotel and turn right in the main street. After 75m a Scottish Rights of Way Society signpost indicates 'Public Footpath to Lair, Glenshee 5' on the left up a driveway. Follow this and after another 30m it becomes a footpath, follow a cutting or groove between high banks.

About 150m from the main road there is a gate and a stile. Cross the stile and turn left at the far side noting the waymarked arrow on a post. Follow the left-hand side of a wall and fence.

A hundred metres from the stile at GR 083603 the path turns slightly to the right after two large rowan trees are passed to our right. Continue alongside the wall and fence, noting the wall at 90 degrees to our left. After the second wall on our left keep straight on across a field drain with a fence to our right and a wall on our left. After 20m there is a stile, after which the wall and fence are on our left.

After 200m we arrive at a wrought iron gate - this is at GR 086605. To the right is a small stand of larch trees. Go over the stile to the right of this gate.

From the top of this stile note the compact plantation slightly to

157

the left and the sparse stand of Scots pine slightly to the right. We aim uphill to the left-hand side of the sparse stand of pine. Ignore rough tracks leading off right and crossing our (vague) path.

As we reach the left-hand side of the pines the first of three marker posts comes into view, as we pass some exposed rocks on the right. A path materialises to skirt round the left-hand side of the pines. As the ground levels head for the far left-hand corner of the plantation that lies behind the sparse group of pines. Here, at GR 094608, is a stile, a gate and a Scottish Rights of Way Society signpost.

Cross the stile and note the stone wall some 200m away on the right. Head across the field in front of you, veering slightly further away from this wall. After a couple of hundred metres a gate and stile and marker post will be seen straight ahead across a fence (this fence is not on the Pathfinder map!) at GR 096610.

From this stile bear right and head down to the signposted bridge over a burn, cross the stile and turn left to skirt round the left side of the next field, noting the right of way markers. We double back in the top corner of the field and with the wall still on the left walk past a gate and then left over a waymarked stile into a small stand of larch and pine at GR 098614.

Walk through, and out of, the trees up the right-hand edge of the field, crossing a stile at GR 099613 by a gate and waymark post. Note the castle grounds on the right. A waymark post confirms the route as a track joins us from the right. We arrive at GR 102615 (reference point 32km/20 miles) at a stile, gate and Scottish Rights of Way Society signpost. Cross the stile, cross the track on the far side, and walk up the track that lies opposite for 75m, after which we cross yet another stile by a gate.

Turn right over this stile (at GR 102616), follow the curving right-hand edge of the field. After 250m and 75m before the fence and stile a track from the castle area joins us on the right. This track is followed to the next gate, stile and signpost at GR 104619, from which point the track is followed to GR 110625 where there is a stile, an iron gate and a marker post.

Cross the stile and follow the track, bearing left for about 200m to a fork.

MAP 7. LAIR

Take the right-hand fork crossing the wall twice before reaching the bridge over the Allt Coirie a' Bhaile. After the footbridge turn right and cross the stile over the wall. The path now follows open moor - keep a

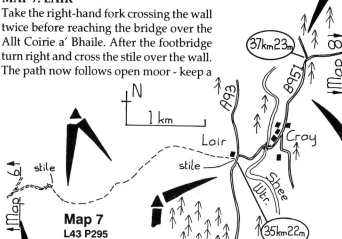

Map 7
L43 P295

sharp eye out for the marker posts which can be seen ahead as we pass over the watershed at GR 128629.

We then descend the right-hand bank of the Allt an Lair to a stile and Scottish Rights of Way Society signpost at GR 142633 (reference point 35km/22 miles) where we emerge on the main road.

Turn left on the A93 for 20m, then right on the B951. There now follows 6km (4 miles) of road walking (sorry!) via reference point 37km (23 miles) where we keep right for Forter. Stepping out, about an hour and a quarter should see it off.

MAP 8. FORTER

At 40km (25 miles) the beautifully restored Forter Castle can be seen as we leave the 'B' road and head towards Little Forter. Turning right at 41km (25.5 miles) we cross the Bridge of Forter noting the track immediately on the left up the 'quiet' side of Glen Isla.

Head south for 100m from the bridge and then turn sharp left up a steep track through a high gate. Take care not to miss this turning.

At 42km (26 miles) the main track doubles back to the right to Auchintaple Loch but we keep on up the hill on the rougher track. Beyond the gate are superb views up Glen Isla - a good stopping

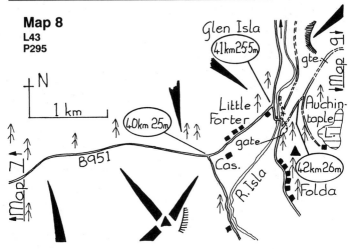

point after that road walk and the steep hill!

We soon crest the hill.

MAP 9. MUCKLE BURN

Beyond the top of the hill are two gates, between which a right turn (at 44km / 27 miles), drops back down to Auchintaple Loch and The Mill. We keep left. After the second gate a rough track is noted

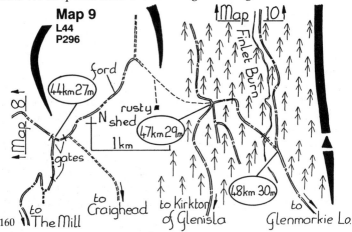

In Glen Clova (Walk 5)
Bridge at Etnach - Glen Tanar (Walk 5)

From the Glen Roy viewpoint (Walk 6)
Coignafearn Lodge (Walk 6)

leading down to Craighead: keep left again.

Our track continues around the head of the Muckle Burn and we ignore yet another turning, this one heading due north and not shown on the O.S. map. Our track, now heading south-east, just about peters out before we enter the forest. The last couple of hundred metres to reference point 47km (29 miles) is no more than a firebreak.

From this complex junction of forest tracks (that is at 47km/29 miles) we head just north of due east, over a low watershed, and cross the Finlet Burn by a concrete bridge just

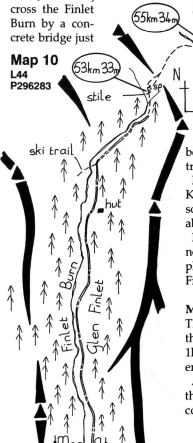

Map 10
L44
P296283

before reaching the main forest track at 48km (30 miles).

Note: If B&B is pre-booked at Kirkton of Glenisla tracks lead south to the road from both the above reference points.

From 48km (30 miles) head north - there follows a long uphill plod through trees alongside the Finlet Burn.

MAP 10. KILBO
The only points of interest are the 'lunch hut' and the ski trail 1km (half a mile) before the track ends.

At the end of the forest track there is little to suggest the route continues. Head due north,

161

dodging between the trees with the Altbuie Burn on the left; this entails crossing a small tributary of the burn.

We suddenly emerge from the trees at reference point 53km (33 miles), at a stile - complete with a Scottish Rights of Way Society signpost.

From here it is all too easy to head north-west to what looks like, but isn't the watershed. Turn right heading north-east - the vague path divides and rejoins through the Glack of Balquhader (the col is not named on the Landranger map but is between Broom Hill and Craigie Thieves).

The path, vague in places, runs north-east then east, dropping into White Glen at the head of Glen Prosen. A gate is found across the end of the Glen Prosen track, a couple of hundred metres above the ruined cottage of Kilbo at 55km (34 miles).

The Kilbo Path, named after the ruin, heads north through the trees for the climb over to Glen Doll.

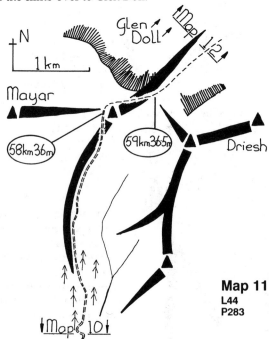

Map 11
L44
P283

MAP 11. MAYAR AND DRIESH

We follow the deteriorating path up Carn Dye and the wonderfully named Shank of Drumwhallow. Care is needed in misty conditions as a nameless summit is reached at GR 253738 - reference point 58km (36 miles).

In clear weather the summit of Mayar lying less than 1.5km (a mile) to the west is within easy reach. Continuing on our path to 59km (36.5 miles) the summit of Driesh may be reached again less than 1.5km from our path but not recommended in mist as the dog-leg route crosses a subsidiary summit first. Good navigation is required to avoid nearby crags.

Our path descends the steep east flank of the equally well named Shank of Drumfollow.

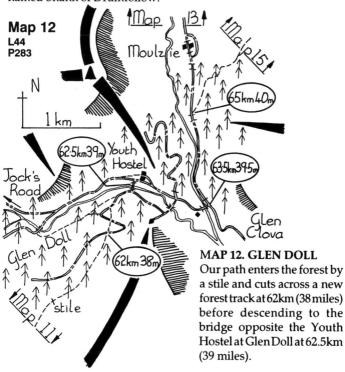

MAP 12. GLEN DOLL

Our path enters the forest by a stile and cuts across a new forest track at 62km (38 miles) before descending to the bridge opposite the Youth Hostel at Glen Doll at 62.5km (39 miles).

The hostel is situated at the start of Jock's Road, an old drovers' route by Glen Callater to Braemar and a committing route with several kilometres of indistinct path around the 900m contour.

Assuming a night's rest is taken at the hostel our route continues down Glen Doll to reach Glen Clova, crossing its river, the South Esk, to arrive among a mass of signposts at 63.5km (39.5 miles).

Here, a left turn takes us into upper Glen Clova: a gate keeps vehicles at bay - the area is very popular with both tourists and walkers.

At 65km (40 miles) a signpost indicates the Mounth Road to Glen Muick. This shorter alternative continues on Map 15. However, the more interesting route (for walkers - not historically) continues up Glen Clova, by-passing Moulzie.

MAP 13. GLEN CLOVA

The way ahead, and the Capel Mounth, were well used routes for drovers heading south from the inn at Spittal of Glenmuick or prior

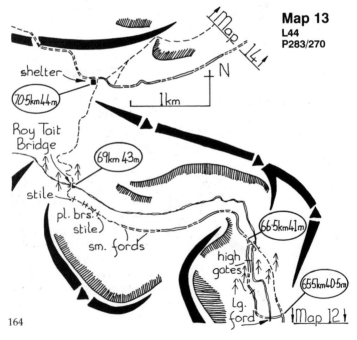

Map 13
L44
P283/270

shelter

70·5km44m

Roy Tait Bridge

69km 43m

stile

pl. brs.
stile

sm. fords

66·5km41m

high gates

655km40·5m

lg. ford

Map 12

to that, the old inn at the Fords of Inchnabobart. Sadly the inns have long gone and not so much as a cup of tea is available at the Spittal.

Our route arrives at a left-hand bend at 65.5km (40.5 miles). Keep straight on here on a rough track that becomes no more than a path: to the left on the main track is a large ford!

A new footbridge brings us back to the main track at 66.5km (41 miles). Soon the track starts to degenerate and becomes a rough path before the Roy Tait Memorial Bridge is reached at 69km (43 miles). Take care not to fall down the waterfall beneath the bridge whilst trying to read the plaque!

The hill path continues to climb, becomes less distinct and arrives at the shelter at 70.5km (44 miles). This is on the Broad Cairn track, its top lying only 1.5km (a mile) WNW,

We turn east, following the high track for the best views, though the good path via Corrie Chash will provide a quicker retreat from rough weather on the plateau.

Map 14. LOCH MUICK
From map 13:

A sharp descent brings the track down to reference point 75km (46.5 miles) where we are joined by the lochside path before the bridge.

The improving track provides easy walking along the lochside to 77.5km (48 miles) where a Scottish

Map 14
L44
P270

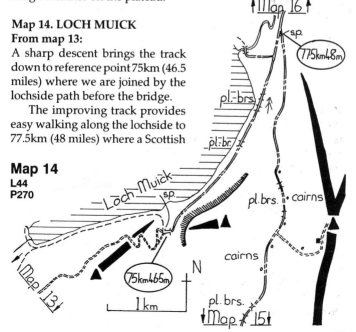

Map 15
L44
P283/270

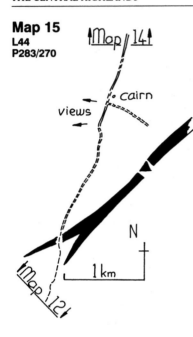

Rights of Way Society signpost indicates the Capel Mounth joining from our right.

From map 15:

A pair of small plank bridges are crossed as the cairned track crosses the plateau. The rough track on the right leads to a simple shelter - too far off the route to be much use as we soon drop steeply above the lochside to join the Broad Cairn track at 77.5km (48 miles).

For those interested in distances (beyond their use as reference points) deduct 5km (3 miles) from now on if you walked over the Capel Mounth.

MAP 15. MOUNTH ROAD

The Capel Mounth 'road' rises from Glen Clova as a steep path but as it arrives on the high, wild plateau it improves to a track, with magnificent views to the west and north - here the vast spread of Lochnagar plateau can be seen.

MAP 16. SPITTAL OF GLENMUICK

We arrive at Spittal of Glenmuick. Spittal, that is, as in hospital or hospice which became hostelry. No pub hereabouts today! Just a visitor centre, a toilet, and a car park - often filled to capacity. Glenmuick is a favourite for day-tripping Aberdonians - as is Glen Tanar.

The right of way continues by the site of another, older, inn at Inchnabobart to Easter Balmoral across the head of Glen Girnock. Drovers also used Glen Gelder and, in summer, the White Mounth

Map 16
L44
P270

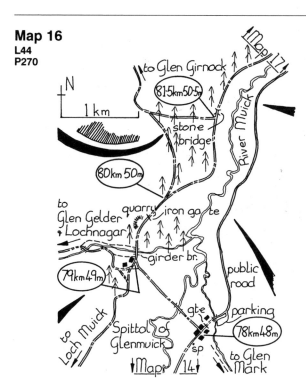

- a direct route almost over the summit of Lochnagar - as a short cut from Braemar via Glen Callater.

We turn left at the Spittal at 78km (48 miles) to cross the Glen to the start of the White Mounth/Lochnagar/Glen Gelder track at 79km (49 miles). A right turn takes us over the Allt na guibhsaich and, by-passing the Glen Girnock track at 80km (50 miles). On to the old inn site and ford (now a bridge) at Inchnabobart at 81.5km (50.5 miles).

An excellent track provides easy walking down Glen Muick.

MAP 17. LINN OF MUICK

The track continues past the site of the old bridge just above the Linn of Muick at 84km (52 miles).

Above, a network of forest tracks runs through the forest but the weary walker will be intent only on heading for Ballater. The Linn of Muick does, however, provide a good excuse for a short rest.

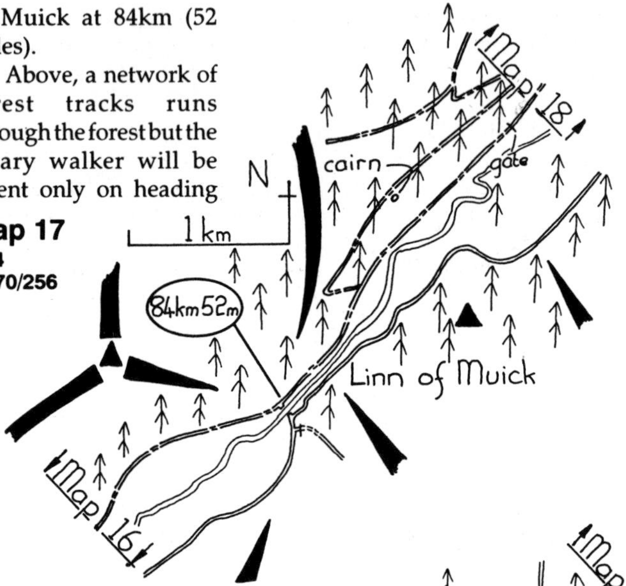

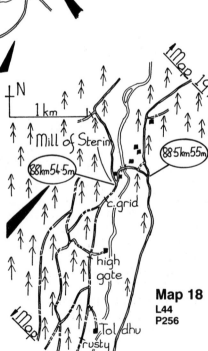

Map 17
L44
P270/256

84km 52m

cairn

gate

Linn of Muick

Map 18
N
1 km

Mill of Sterin

88km 54.5m

88.5km 55m

c.grid

high gate

Tol dhu

rusty gate

Map 18
L44
P256

MAP 18. MILL OF STERIN

Ignoring all left and right turns the track arrives at the public road at Mill of Sterin at 88km (54.5 miles). From here 4.5km / 3 miles of road walking takes us into Ballater. Take a right turn at Mill

168

of Sterin, then over the bridge and a steep climb (ouch!) to 88.5km (55 miles) where a left turn takes us in a north-easterly direction for Ballater.

MAP 19. BALLATER

The minor road emerges at Bridge of Muick at 91.5km (56.5 miles). The 'B' road leads us to the bridge across the Dee into Ballater at 92.5km (57 miles). What a pity there is no longer a Youth Hostel here

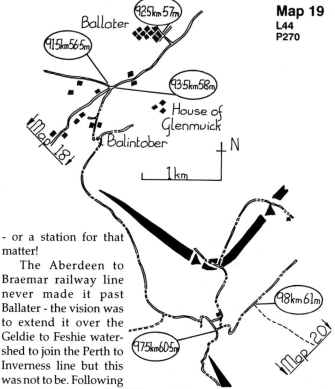

Map 19
L44
P270

- or a station for that matter!

The Aberdeen to Braemar railway line never made it past Ballater - the vision was to extend it over the Geldie to Feshie watershed to join the Perth to Inverness line but this was not to be. Following its inevitable closure the Ballater to Dinnet section is now a cycleway and walkway, providing an alternative route to the start of picturesque Glen Tanar.

169

However, after a night's rest and back at Bridge of Muick at 93.5km (58 miles) our route now follows the old drovers' road to the head of Glen Tanar.

Take the track to the left of the monument just before Bridge of Muick, keeping left after 300m to by-pass the house at Balintober. Round the bend, through a gate and right through another gate takes us onto the hill track.

At the complex assortment of tracks around reference point 97.5km (60.5 miles) follow the signpost to 'Mount Keen', dropping into the wild glen of the Pollagach Burn before climbing again from another signpost at reference point 98km (61 miles) over the hill of Lach na Gualainn for Glen Tanar.

MAP 20. SHIEL OF GLENTANAR

The footpath continues to drop down the hillside to what was an

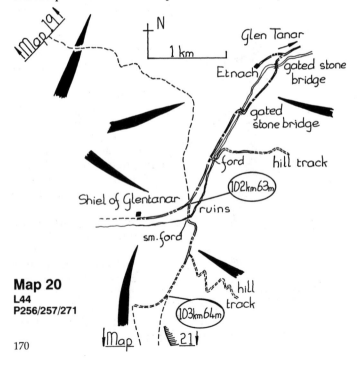

Map 20
L44
P256/257/271

important crossroads in the head of Glen Tanar at 102km (63 miles). Now a very remote place indeed, the ruins hereabouts included an inn where the drovers rested for the night before tackling the Mounth Road by Mount Keen.

The Shiel of Glentanar, a kilometre up the glen, was until quite recently a bothy, but after a fire this has now been partially demolished.

Here we are joined by the old road from Dinnet and Aboyne which joins us via Glen Tanar before our climb to the Capel Mounth. A ford marks the start of the climb and rough tracks, firstly on the left and secondly on the right, are by-passed as the route, now a walkers' path, climbs steeply.

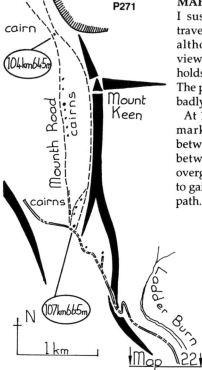

Map 21
L44
P271

MAP 21. MOUNT KEEN

I suspect many will wish to traverse Mount Keen, however although an outstanding viewpoint the Mounth Road holds more interest historically. The paths over Mount Keen are badly eroded.

At 104km (64.5 miles) a cairn marks the narrowest point between two paths. The gap between, only 10m wide, is overgrown and has to be crossed to gain the lower Mounth Road path. Be careful as neither path is clearly visible from the other.

The Mounth Road appears at first glance to be just a single-width walkers' path but it is clear that it was once excavated to a width of nearly 2m. This was the main road of long ago -

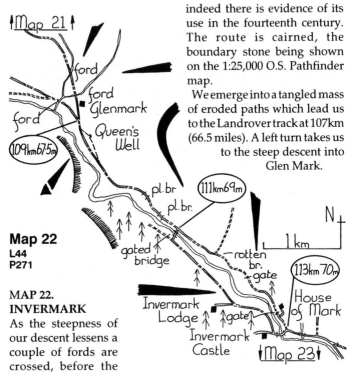

indeed there is evidence of its use in the fourteenth century. The route is cairned, the boundary stone being shown on the 1:25,000 O.S. Pathfinder map.

We emerge into a tangled mass of eroded paths which lead us to the Landrover track at 107km (66.5 miles). A left turn takes us to the steep descent into Glen Mark.

Map 22
L44
P271

MAP 22.
INVERMARK

As the steepness of our descent lessens a couple of fords are crossed, before the cottage at Glenmark. The Glen Mark track is joined at 109km (67.5 miles). A few metres after this a path diverts left to the Queen's Well, an elaborate stone arched structure marking the well said to have been used by Queen Victoria on one of her many expeditions in the Highlands. It is still a good excuse to rest weary feet!

The track descends to reference point 111km (69 miles) at which point the main track crosses the Water of Mark. However, we stay on the north-east bank of the Water of Mark on the now deteriorating track which eventually improves again to emerge on the public road at 113km (70 miles).

Here the short diversion for a closer look at Invermark Castle, built in 1526, is worthwhile.

Queen's Well

MAP 23. RIVER NORTH ESK

From Invermark Castle to Tarfside is a road walk of some 7km (4.5 miles). However, an hour and a half of steady walking should see it off, and the way ahead is pleasant - I can think of many worse roads to walk on!

Tarfside marks the start of two 'roads' that divide high on the hill, the Fungle and Firmounth roads. These two ancient ways, and the other Mounth Roads, linked the crossing points of the Dee (when these were just fords) with the routes south to the cattle markets.

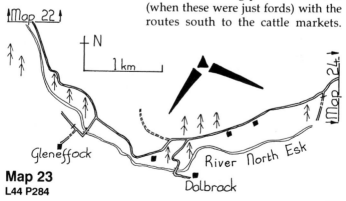

Map 23
L44 P284

Wheeled transport was not used therefore the steep climbs were not such an issue - it was more important to gain higher, dry ground.

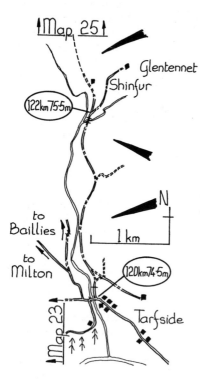

MAP 24. TARFSIDE

Departing Tarfside at 120km (74.5 miles) a good track heads north up the east bank of Water of Tarf. Keep left at the turning to Glentennet at 122km (75.5 miles). The track becomes a path soon after passing Shinfur.

There is some debate as to whether the Fungle or Firmounth road was the original route, it is however well documented that both were well used by both cattle drovers and cattle thieves. Indeed, Invermark Castle was built as part of an attempt to control cattle thieving which appeared to be quite an industry.

The route by-passes the cottage at Shinfur and commences the steady climb.

Map 24
L44
P284/271

Map 25
L44
P271

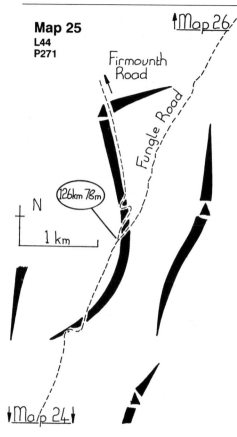

Firmounth Road

Fungle Road

126km 78m

N

1 km

↑Map 26↑

↑Map 24↓

MAP 25. FUNGLE ROAD

The path climbs the southern spur of Tampie until the ways divide at reference point 126km (78 miles). This 'road junction', at least 600 years old, marks the divergence of the Firmounth Road over Tampie and into the lower reaches of Glen Tanar.

Our route, the Fungle Road, keeps right at this point and rises across the hillside only a short distance to a lower watershed before the path deteriorates somewhat on its descent to Birse.

MAP 26. BIRSE

The descending path becomes a rough track and reaches a gate which marks the enclosed land around the farm at Ballochan and the restored (but private) castle of Birse.

Here an attempt has been made to signpost a diversion to the right of way around the west side of Birse Castle, however the going is far from straightforward.

A left turn before the gate, at 131km (81 miles), takes us over boggy ground with a fence on top of a wall on our right. A decrepit plank bridge and a stile confirm the way as in places we have to

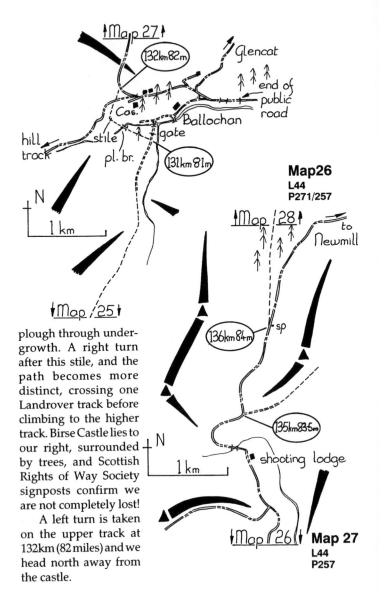

132km 82m

Glencat

end of
public
road

Ballochan

Cos.

gate

hill
track

stile

pl. br.

131km 81m

Map26
L44
P271/257

N

1 km

↑Map /28↑

to
Newmill

↓Map /25↓

136km 84m

sp

135km 83.5m

plough through under-
growth. A right turn
after this stile, and the
path becomes more
distinct, crossing one
Landrover track before
climbing to the higher
track. Birse Castle lies to
our right, surrounded
by trees, and Scottish
Rights of Way Society
signposts confirm we
are not completely lost!

A left turn is taken
on the upper track at
132km (82 miles) and we
head north away from
the castle.

N

1 km

shooting lodge

↓Map /26↓

Map 27
L44
P257

176

MAP 27. FUNGLE ROAD (N)

The track climbs above The Gwaves, a steep ravine: the hill track on the left is by-passed. A rather grand shooting lodge is passed but does not provide any shelter for the walker (unless the rain is horizontal!) and a loop in the track takes us around the head of the Burn of Auldgarney which rushes through The Gwaves.

Ignoring the rough track heading east from reference point 135km (83.5 miles) we head north.

Arriving at 136km (84 miles) note the path on the left is taken. Despite it being a clear path of considerable importance this is not shown on the O.S. Landranger map! Both this and the continuing track to Newmill (despite the signposts) are rights of way. This path is followed to The Guard.

MAP 28. ABOYNE

The path becomes a rough track before The Guard - a cottage in a remote and secluded location. The main access to The Guard goes off on the left but we head straight on - north - dropping down to The Fungle.

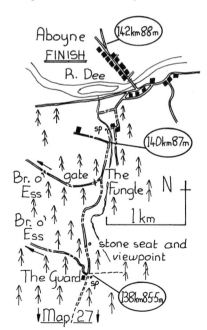

Our last place for a short rest is the Rest and be Thankful seat built by William C Brooks, laird of Glentanar who, thankfully for the many walkers who stop here, had a passion for building monuments.

We press on keeping the burn - Allt Dinnie - on the right. The way becomes a path at 140km

Map 28
L44 P257

(87 miles), turning right over the burn at a Scottish Rights of Way Society signpost. A track is picked up which takes us north and east, onto metalled roads and into the pleasant town of Aboyne, the end of our trek at 142km (88 miles).

Here, a regular bus service runs to Aberdeen for the train home.

Roy Tait Memorial Bridge

WALK 6:
Across the Monadhliath

This walk explores the vast area of remote country known as the Monadhliath Mountains. It is an area little frequented by the walker as it is not peppered with Munros - other than the notable exception of Creag Meagaidh and its near neighbours, and a few isolated tops above Newtonmore, all of which are on the south-eastern edge of the Monadhliath.

The remainder of the area comprises high moorland. Many of the tops are just under the magic 3000ft (914m), which would give Munro status - and the associated attention of hillwalkers - to these remote hills.

The area is penetrated, but not intersected, by some superb glens - Glen Roy, the start of this walk, Glen Gloy, the Findhorn, Dulnain and Strath Nairn. The heart of the region gives rise to the River Spey which

Walk 6: Across the Monadhliath

Gradient profile: Across the Monadhliath

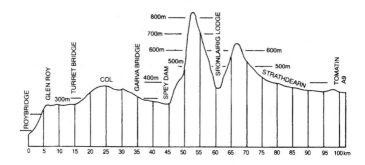

flows into the North Sea at Spey Bay beyond Lossiemouth - or most of it does! At Spey Dam some of its headwater is diverted to the Treig-Laggan hydro scheme - bound for Fort William and encountered on Walk 3 of this book.

The walk involves some road-walking in Glen Roy, around Spey Dam and around Tomatin, and some pathless moor - requiring good navigation skills, and fitness for the climb out of Glen Markie. The rewards are a long hike through an unfrequented region. It is perhaps unfortunate that it is not possible to include the Corrieyairack Pass and the Dulnain into the walk, though the Corrieyairack

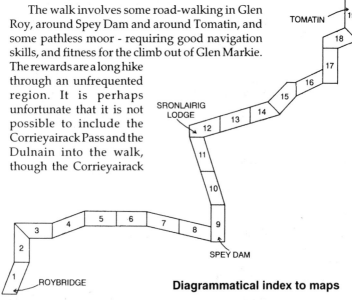

Diagrammatical index to maps

is marred by rusting pylons and the possible return of vehicular traffic (it is a public road at the time of writing, impassable even to 4x4s).

There is a railway station at the start and a bus stop at the finish - note the bus stops on the A9, not in Tomatin.

Accommodation has to be carried. There are bothies but Melgarve especially should be avoided as it suffers from over-use. Be prepared to camp wild throughout.

Public roads are encountered at Spey Dam, 3km (2 miles) north, off the route, of Sronlairig Lodge, and from Coignafearn Old Lodge by the Findhorn.

Access to Creag Meagaidh is possible from Glen Roy, indeed this is the preferred route for me, avoiding the tramp with the crowds up the boardwalk from Laggan. It is however a hard, committing route, wild and mostly pathless.

Walk 6: Across the Monadhliath - at a glance guide

Length: 102.5km (63.5 miles) - plus a mile to the bus! 4-6 days

Total climbing: approximately 1200m

Accommodation: Wild camping (plus possible bothies)

Roads at: Roybridge 0km to
Brae Roy Lodge 14.5km (9 miles)
Garva Bridge 36.5km (22.5 miles) to
Spey Dam 44km (27.5 miles)
Sronlairig Lodge 61km (38 miles) (2km north off route)
Coignafearn Old Lodge 83km (51.5 miles)
Dalmigavie Lodge 92km (57 miles) to
Tomatin 102.5km (63.5 miles)

Bus services at: Roybridge 0km
Tomatin 102.5km (63.5 miles) (1 mile north on A9)

Rail services at: Roybridge 0km

Access to mountain groups en route:
Creag Meagaidh
Geal Charn

O.S. maps (in their order of appearance):
Landranger 34, 35*
Pathfinder 265, 251, 252, 239, 223**, 224, 209, 210*
* the bus stop is just off the map to the north on the A9
** only for 300m!

MAP 1. ROYBRIDGE

Starting from the railway station at Roybridge, head west for some 400m on the A86, crossing the River Roy then immediately right up the minor road up Glen Roy.

Road walking is often

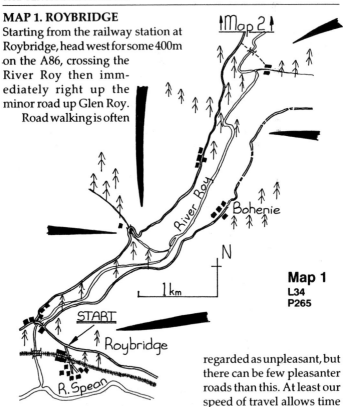

Map 1
L34
P265

regarded as unpleasant, but there can be few pleasanter roads than this. At least our speed of travel allows time to fully appreciate the famous parallel roads - not roads at all but the shore lines of an ice-dammed loch of 10,000 years ago. Why the Ordnance Survey choose to depict this unique geographical feature as an 'other road, drive or track' baffles me - and leads to a confusing representation of the upper glen.

MAP 2. GLEN ROY

At reference point 6km (4 miles) the car park and viewpoint provides a good excuse for a rest. There is an information panel explaining the parallel roads and a superb view back down to Glen

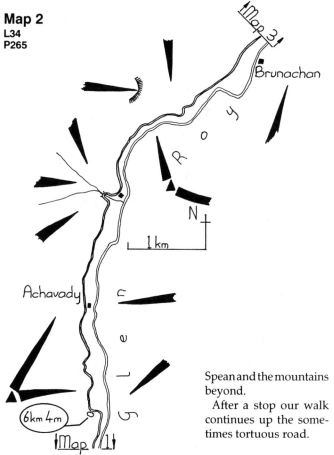

Map 2
L34
P265

Brunachan

R o y

N

1 km

Achavady

G l e n

6km 4m

Map 1

Spean and the mountains beyond.

After a stop our walk continues up the sometimes tortuous road.

MAP 3. TURRET BRIDGE

At last the road ends - at Brae Roy Lodge, 14.5km (9 miles) from the start. We walk between the lodge buildings, passing through a gate, and turn sharp right over Turret Bridge. The track joining us from the left comes over from Glen Gloy - this is a right of way but the path, though clearly visible, is not on the O.S. map.

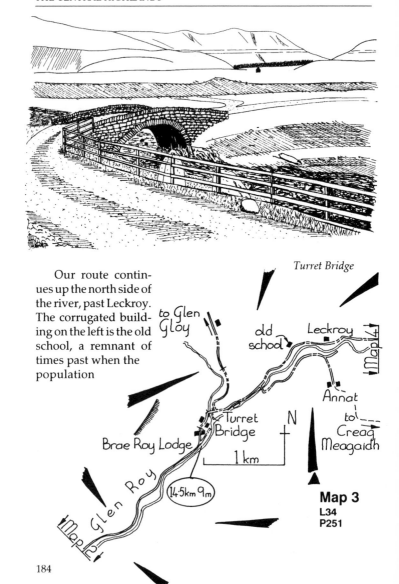

Turret Bridge

Our route continues up the north side of the river, past Leckroy. The corrugated building on the left is the old school, a remnant of times past when the population

to Glen Gloy

old school

Leckroy

Map 4

Turret Bridge

Annat

to Creag Meagaidh

N

Brae Roy Lodge

1 km

Glen Roy

14·5km 9m

Map 2

Map 3
L34
P251

of the glens was sufficient to require a school. The upper glens are far more remote now than they were even 100 years ago and even then far less populated than in the pre-clearance times of the eighteenth century.

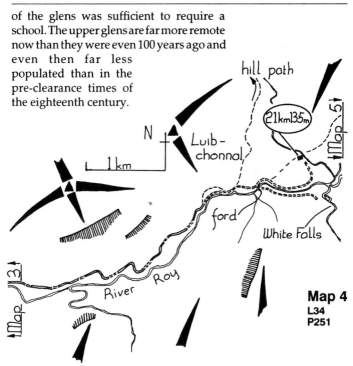

MAP 4. LUIB-CHONNAL

Beyond Leckroy the track climbs and becomes rougher as we rise almost to the level of the lowest 'parallel road'. These lie at 261m, 326m and 350m as the height of the ice-dam varied.

Eventually the bothy at Luib-chonnal is reached - either by following the rough track which follows the riverbank or cutting across a flat grassy area on a somewhat vague path. The bothy is 21km (13.5 miles) from Roybridge and occupies a superb setting opposite White Falls. Information in the bothy gives us insight into the glen in times past. The bothy must, of course, be treated with absolute respect.

Beyond the bothy the path, soon becoming vague, is reached by fording the Allt Chonnal.

Luib-chonnal

MAP 5. SHESGNAN

The path, now becoming faint, crosses the watershed - marked as 'col' on the O.S. map. The term 'Col' is not usually used in Scotland - more usually described as a 'bealach' - however this flat watershed is described as Col by name at 24km (15 miles). It is indeed a significant place for beyond here all drains into the Spey. To our

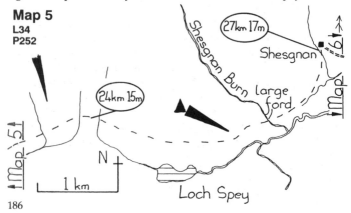

186

right is Loch Spey below which the burns join to form an already sizeable river. The vague path continues to cross the Shesgnan Burn, which can be troublesome if in spate. After a couple of smaller fords the ruin at Shesgnan is reached at 27km (17 miles), this providing only temporary shelter from the weather.

Beyond Shesgnan an improving track leads to Melgarve.

MAP 6. MELGARVE

The Allt Yairack is bridged as the track leads us to Melgarve at 30km (19 miles). The bothy is at the junction with the Corrieyairack Pass. I repeat my discouragement of its use as a bothy, especially in summer - it is just too accessible.

The Corrieyairack Pass is a public road, once a drove road from Cannich via Glen Moriston and crossing the Great Glen at Fort Augustus, continuing to join the A9 route at Dalwhinnie. The route was built up to Military Road standard in 1731 and used for both military purposes and for the movement of cattle until the droving trade died out around 1880.

The road 'enjoyed' public road status but much damage resulted from over-use by 4x4 enthusiasts. A recent flood washed out the Fort Augustus end, making it impassable, but moves are afloat to reinstate it for 4x4 use - surely a retrograde step in trying to keep our

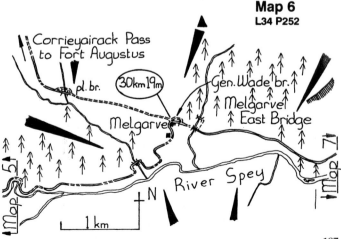

Map 6
L34 P252

Corrieyairack Pass to Fort Augustus

pl. br.

30km 19m

Gen. Wade br.

Melgarve

Melgarve East Bridge

Melgarve

Map 5

Map 7

N   River Spey

1 km

Melgarve East Bridge

wild places wild.

A short diversion to Melgarve East Bridge is worth it as the road has been realigned and this now lies at the edge of the wood 100m or so off the route.

From here the road, now metalled, heads east.

MAP 7. GARVA BRIDGE
Prior to Garva Bridge the glen has, in my opinion, been spoilt by the unnatural hard-edged conifer plantations. The glen without these plantations would present a wild scene indeed but the ugly blocks of dark conifers, seemingly planted at random, together with the line of pylons, demonstrate how we can so easily spoil the scene. Perhaps the trees could have been used to partly hide the pylons?

The road continues to Garva Bridge at 36.5km (22.5 miles). This is a superb example of one of the larger bridges built by General Wade and marks the end of the public road 'proper'.

MAP 8. LOCH CRUNACHDAN
Garvamore is soon passed - here the buildings sadly being left to ruin were formerly a barracks and later an inn. We continue on the

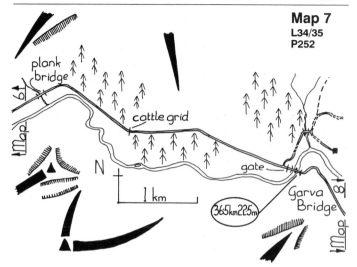

Map 7
L34/35
P252

plank bridge · Map 6 · cattle grid · N · 1 km · gate · 365km 225m · Garva Bridge · Map 8

road, crossing the man-made waterway at the end of Glen Shirra at 41km (25.5 miles). The embankments form part of the Spey Dam behind which the reservoir taps into the Spey and the Markie Burn, stealing some of the water bound for the North Sea and diverting it into Loch Laggan for the Fort William aluminium works hydro scheme. Spey Dam was completed in 1943, the final phase of the hydro scheme which had commenced in 1926. The earthworks still

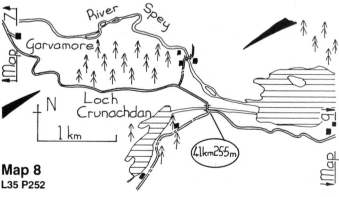

Map 7 · River Spey · Garvamore · Map 6 · N · Loch Crunachdan · 1 km · 41km 255m · Map 9 · Map 8

Map 8
L35 P252

look unnatural despite over 50 years since their construction.

A stroll along the southern edge of the reservoir brings us to the end of the road section.

MAP 9. SPEY DAM

The road swings left below Spey Dam and at 44km (27.5 miles), where the road bends sharply right, we turn left, pass through a gate and walk directly towards the dam. The track turns right to head for Glen Markie.

The next section of the walk, from Glen Markie (Spey Dam) to Glen Markie (Sronlairig) is a wild, committing walk. The climb up out of Glen Markie is not for the faint-hearted and it is probably best to camp in Glen Markie and tackle the climb refreshed and full of porridge in the morning!

We head north through the several gates up the main Glen Markie track.

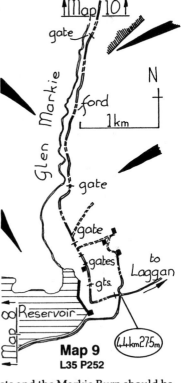

Map 9
L35 P252

MAP 10. GEAL CHARN

The track extends a little further than the O.S. map suggests and the Markie Burn should be forded at GR 588982. Follow the path due north for about 300m to reference point 50km (31 miles). The right of way then heads north-west, steeply, to the end of a flat broad ridge at GR 583990.

Follow the ridge north-west up a short, steeper section around GR 580993, then flat ground, then a gradual climb to cross the broad, wild ridge of high ground around GR 570000. From here Geal Charn is easily accessible to the south-west, about 1.5km (a mile) away. Great care should be taken in this area regarding navigation.

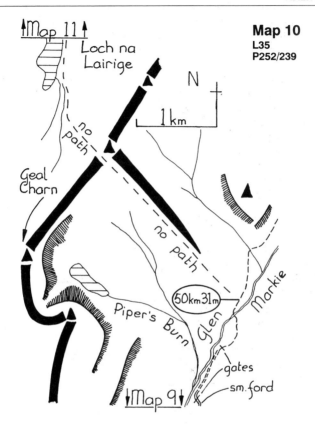

Map 10
L35
P252/239

Map 11

Loch na Lairige

no path

Geal Charn

no path

50km31m

Piper's Burn

Glen Markie

gates

sm.ford

Map 9

N

1 km

Returning to GR 570000 head NNW and follow one of the burns down to Loch na Lairige, then head north up its east shore.

(Note: if heading north from Geal Charn summit in mist beware of following the wrong burn - from GR 563992 which turns west, then south-west - back to Garva Bridge!)

MAP 11. CHALYBEATE SPRING
Once Loch na Lairige is reached continue north following the east bank of the burn flowing from it. After a few minor fords a stalkers'

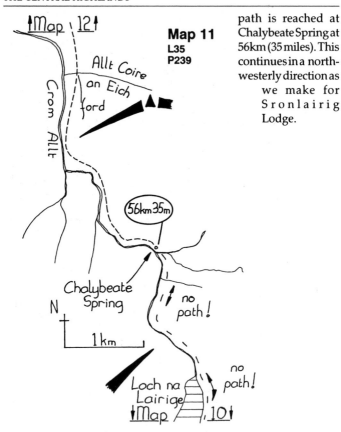

path is reached at Chalybeate Spring at 56km (35 miles). This continues in a north-westerly direction as we make for Sronlairig Lodge.

Map 11
L35
P239

MAP 12. SRONLAIRIG LODGE

Our path runs into a forest track as the descent to the lodge is made.

Sronlairig Lodge at 61km (38 miles) was once a magnificent building: now in a ruinous state it looks like a set for a horror film. Take heed of the 'Do not enter' signs! What a place this must have been in its heyday!

We turn right at the junction between the two bridges and then immediately right again to pick up the footpath above the gorge of the Glenmarkie Burn.

Sronlairig Lodge

At 63 km (39 miles) a rough track continues ahead. However, we strike left up a groove to the left of a drumlin to gain the continuation of the now almost non-existent path. Our position

Map 12
L35
P239

ruined bothy

iron gate posts

Glen Markie

to Loch Killin and Stratherrick

63km 39m

61km 38m

Glenmarkie Burn

N

1 km

ruin

Sronlairig Lo.

Allt Cam Ban

↓Map 11↓

Map 12→

is confirmed a little further up the glen by a pair of iron gateposts, 200m

193

Ruined Bothy - Glen Markie

beyond which is a ruined
bothy to the right.

MAP 13. MARKIE/
FINDHORN WATER-
SHED

The route continues up
Glen Markie, becoming
pathless in the upper
reaches, though traces of old

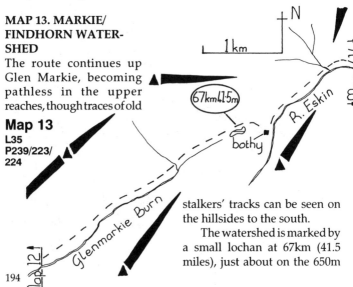

Map 13
L35
**P239/223/
224**

stalkers' tracks can be seen on
the hillsides to the south.

The watershed is marked by
a small lochan at 67km (41.5
miles), just about on the 650m

contour. Our route turns south to the almost ruinous bothy, which still just about provides emergency shelter, at 67km (41.5 miles), at the side of the Allt Coire an t-Sreatha. This is effectively the infant River Eskin - which becomes the River Findhorn, keeping up the Scottish tradition of rivers undergoing an identity crisis in their upper reaches!

Faint paths and knee-deep heather improve to a rough track, whilst the feeling of isolation is complete.

MAP 14. RIVER ESKIN
Our rough track follows the Eskin, past a superb series of waterfalls. All around lies some of the least-frequented land in Scotland - north to Strath Nairn and south to the Spey and east to the Dulnain - nothing but heather and grouse. Not a hillwalker in sight! Magic!

At 74km (46 miles) a track joins us on the right - across a bridge. This runs to an equally remote dead-end glen at the side of the Abhainn Cro Chlach.

We continue north-east to Dalbeg.

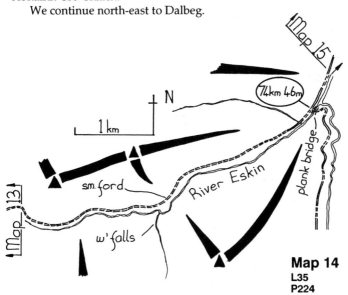

N

1 km

sm. ford

River Eskin

plank bridge

Map 15

74km 46m

Map 13

w' falls

Map 14
L35
P224

MAP 15. DALBEG

Dalbeg at 75km (46.5 miles) is approached either by a ford, or by taking the diversionary path up the side stream to the bridge over the Allt Creagach. Dalbeg was, on my last visit, a locked but windowless shelter used as a feed-store.

The track improves at Dalbeg as the branch tracks up the Allt Creagach, behind Dalbeg, and the Elrick Burn are by-passed.

Gates and cattle grids guard the magnificent Coignafearn Lodge, a beautiful building in a superb setting.

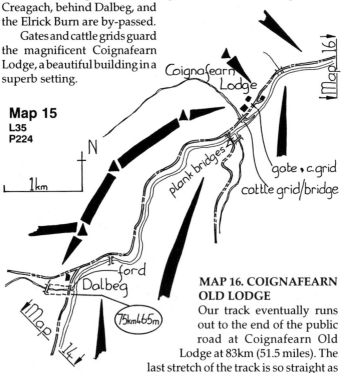

Map 15
L35
P224

MAP 16. COIGNAFEARN OLD LODGE

Our track eventually runs out to the end of the public road at Coignafearn Old Lodge at 83km (51.5 miles). The last stretch of the track is so straight as to hint at military origins but neither drovers nor the building of military roads penetrated the Monadhliath other than over the Corrieyairack Pass.

The road is followed for a mile to the bridge on the branch track on our right at 85km (52.5 miles). Here it is worth some trouble to gain the track on the south-east side of the Findhorn.

If rivers are low follow the track to Coignafeuinternich, cross the bridge and pass through the corner of the wood by gates. The buildings are ruins. Follow the edge of the wood due east to point Z, ignoring the tracks rising up the hillside. Skilful boulder-hopping will effect a crossing - but note this crossing point can be dangerous in spate.

If rivers are high leave the road at reference point 85km (52.5 miles), cross the bridge and go immediately left to follow the bank of the Findhorn. There is a high fence on our right. After about 50m the Allt Fionndairnich is crossed at what should be a shallow ford. Continue to Point X at the north end of the upstream island in the Allt Mhuilin. Here a boulder hop or long shallow paddle will effect a crossing.

The only other alternative is to scramble down into the gorge - boulder hop at Point Y and scramble up the other side.

From the burn it is easy to gain the track and turn left (north).

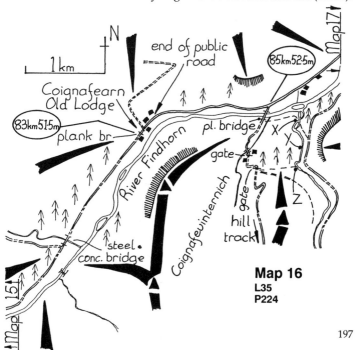

Map 16
L35
P224

MAP 17. CREAG DHUBH

Many of Scotland's glens - especially where rivers are considerable - have a road up each side, each providing access and avoiding the difficulty of bridging the main river. Sometimes both develop into roads but more usually only one does and the other side of the glen suffers due to poorer access. The Findhorn is one such glen but the 'old' road often gives us a picture of life before the surfaced roads, besides providing walkers and cyclists with a more interesting alternative.

Our track is dominated by Creag Dhubh as we wend our way down the now virtually level glen. It is surprising that we are still over 350m above sea level.

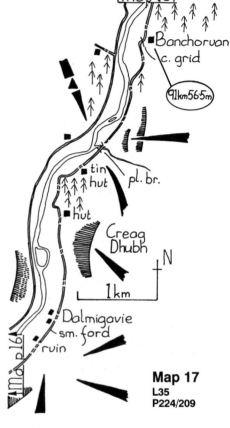

The track improves after Dalmigavie as we follow it past Banchoruan.

MAP 18. DALMIGAVIE LODGE

The track emerges at Dalmigavie Lodge at 92km (57 miles), where there is a bridged link to the public road. However, the more

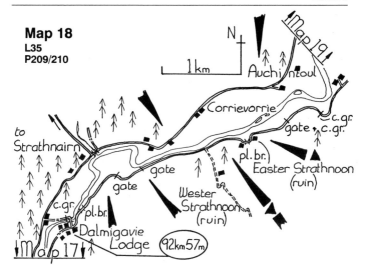

Map 18
L35
P209/210

N

1 km

Auchintoul

Corrievorrie

c.gr.
gate c.gr.

to
Strathnairn

gate

Easter Strathnoon
(ruin)

pl.br.

gate

gate

Wester
Strathnoon
(ruin)

c.gr.
pl.br.

Dalmigavie
Lodge 92km 57m

interesting route continues past Wester Strathnoon and Easter
Strathnoon (sounding very much like the wild west!)

Beyond Dalmigavie we are on a metalled surface once again as
our secondary route continues down Strathdearn. It will be apparent
now that this is an exceptionally long glen!

MAP 19. TOMATIN

The point at which our metalled farm road becomes a public road
is unclear but we eventually emerge at a road junction at reference
point 100km (62 miles). Here, after days in the wild, we are confronted
by the old A9 (which we have just arrived at), the railway, and the
new A9.

We turn left across Findhorn Bridge, on the old A9, reminded of
the days when the drive from Perth to Inverness took the best part
of a day. We arrive in Tomatin at 102.5km (63.5 miles), where an
array of bridges carry old and new roads and railway over the
Findhorn and each other.

I conclude with a reminder. The buses keep to the A9 and stop
at lay-bys at the north end of the loop of old A9 through Tomatin,
just off the edge of the O.S. map!

Map 19
L35
P210

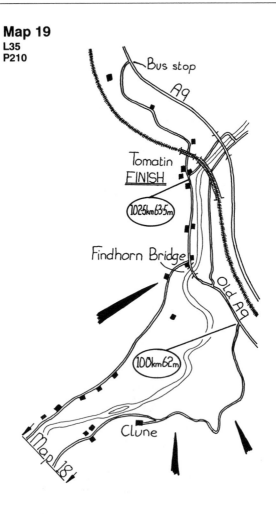

APPENDIX

PUBLIC TRANSPORT
Buses
Scottish Cituylink Agents:

Edinburgh	-	Scottish Citylink Travel Centre
		St Andrew Square Bus Station
Glasgow	-	Scottish Citylink Travel Centre
		Buchanan Bus Station
Aviemore	-	Tourist Information Centre
		Grampian Road
Stirling	-	Stirling Council Travel Office
		Goosecroft Bus Station
Inverness	-	Highland Scottish Omnibuses
		Farraline Park Bus Station
Perth	-	Scottish Citylink Travel Centre
		Leonard Street Bus Station
Pitlochry	-	Tourist Information Centre
		22 Atholl Road

Citylink General Enquiries: 0990 50 50 50

Postbus Timetables:

North East Scotland Postcode AB ZE
Central Fife,
Perthshire & Tayside Postcode DD FK KY PH

Available from: Communications
Royal Mail Scotland & Northern Ireland
102 West Port
Edinburgh EH3 9HS

Rail

Train information:	Inverness	0345 212282
	Scotrail	01463 230961
	Inter City	East Coast 01904 522682

Important note: If you go by car and intend leaving it for more than a couple of days, tell the local police and fill in a route card or you will have half of Scotland out searching for you!

TOURIST INFORMATION CENTRES
(FOR ACCOMMODATION)

	Walk No.		*Walk No.*

Aberdeen — 5
St Nicholas House
Broad Street AB9 1DE
01224 632727
Jan-Dec

Aberfeldy — 4
The Square
01887 820276
Jan-Dec

Aberfoyle — 4
Main Street
01877 382352
April-Oct

Aboyne — 5
Ballater Road Car Park
013398 86060
Easter-Oct

Aviemore — 2 & 6
Grampian Road
Inverness-shire PH22 1PP
01479 810363
Jan-Dec

Ballachulish — 3
Argyll
01855 811296
April-Oct

Ballater — 5
Station Square
013397 55306
Easter-end Oct

Balloch — 4
Balloch Road
01389 753533
March-Nov

Banchory — 5
Bridge Street AB31 3SX
01330 822000
Jan-Dec

Blairgowrie — 5
26 Wellmeadow
01250 872960/873701
Jan-Dec

Braemar — 2
The Mews
Mar Road
013397 41600
Jan-Dec

Brechin — 5
St Ninians Place
01356 623050
April-Sept

Callander — 4
Rob Roy & Trossachs
Visitor Centre
Ancaster Square
01877 330784
March-Dec

	Walk No.		*Walk No.*
Crieff	4		
Town Hall		Kingussie	6
High Street		King Street	
01764 652578		Inverness-shire	
Jan-Dec		01540 661297	
		May-Sept	
Daviot Wood	6		
A9 By Inverness		Oban	1
01463 772203		Argyll Square	
April-Oct		Argyll PA34 4AR	
		01631 563122	
Drymen	4	Jan-Dec	
Drymen Library			
The Square		Pitlochry	1,2,5
01360 660068		22 Atholl Road	
May-Sept		01796 472215/472751	
		Jan-Dec	
Dunkeld	4 & 5		
The Cross		Ralia	1
01350 727688		A9 North by Newtonmore	
March-Oct		Inverness-shire	
		01540 673253	
Fort Augustus	6	April-Oct	
Car Park			
Inverness-shire		Spean Bridge	3 & 6
01320 366367		Inverness-shire	
April-Oct		01397 712576	
		April-Oct	
Fort William	3 & 6		
Cameron Square		Tomintoul	2
Inverness-shire PH33 6AJ		The Square	
01397 703781		01807 580285	
Jan-Dec		April-Nov	
Killin	4	Tyndrum	1 & 3
Main Street		Main Street	
01567 820254		01838 400246	
March-Dec		April-Oct	

Other useful addresses:
Scottish Rights of Way Society Ltd
John Cotton Business Centre
10/2 Sunnyside
Edinburgh
EH7 5RA   Tel: 0131 652 2937

Scottish Youth Hostels Association
7 Glebe Crescent
Stirling
FK8 2JA   Tel: 01786 451181

The Mountaineering Council of Scotland
4a St Catherine's Road
Perth
PH1 5SE   Tel: 01738 638227

The Scottish Landowners' Federation
25 Maritime Street
Edinburgh
EH6 5PW   Tel: 0131 555 1031

Scottish Natural Heritage
12 Hope Terrace
Edinburgh
EH9 2AS   Tel: 0131 447 4784

BIBLIOGRAPHY

Grampian Ways by Robert Smith (ISBN 870978 40 4)

Scottish Hill Tracks, Scottish Rights of Way Society
(ISBN 0-9502811-5-8)

Heading for the Scottish Hills, The Mountaineering Council of Scotland
and The Scottish Landowners' Federation
(ISBN 0-907521-24-X)

The Military Roads in Scotland by William Taylor
(ISBN 1-899863-08-7)

The Drove Roads of Scotland by A.R.B. Haldane (ISBN 1-874744-76-9)

*The Regional History of the Railways of Gt Britain - Volume 15 - North
of Scotland* by John Thomas & David Turnock
(ISBN 0-946537-03-8)

The Callander & Oban Railway by John Thomas (ISBN ?????)

The Killin Branch Railway by Colin Hogarth (ISBN 1-870542-24-X)

Exploring Scottish Hill Tracks by Ralph Storer (ISBN 0 7515 1355 X)

The Cairngorms by Adam Watson (ISBN 0 907521 19 3)

The Munros by Donald Bennet (ISBN 0-907521-31-2)

The Central Highlands by Peter Hodgkiss (ISBN 0-907521-44-4)

Notes